Calvinism and the Capitalist Spirit

Calvinism and the Capitalist Spirit

Max Weber's *Protestant Ethic*

Gianfranco Poggi

The University of Massachusetts Press   Amherst, 198

First published in the United States of America by
THE UNIVERSITY OF MASSACHUSETTS PRESS
Amherst, Massachusetts

Printed in Hong Kong

LC 83–40103

ISBN 0–87023–417–X (cloth)
ISBN 0–87023–418–8 (pbk)

Library of Congress Cataloging in Publication Data

Poggi, Gianfranco.
  Calvinism and the capitalist spirit.

  Includes index.
    1. Weber, Max, 1864–1920. Protestantische Ethik
und der Geist des Kapitalismus. 2. Religion and
sociology. 3. Christian ethics. 4. Capitalism—
Religious aspects—Protestant churches. I. Title.
BR115.E3W436   1984   261.8′5   83–40103
ISBN 0–87023–417–X
ISBN 0–87023–418–8 (pbk.)

Contents

To Pat and Maria

Foreword

Gianfranco Poggi's book is scholarly, dense and written with modesty of tone. It also covers a theme that is very well worn within sociology. Given this, its importance and originality might escape many casual readers. It challenges the basis of our conventional understanding of Max Weber's theory and methodology, and in so doing undermines received notions concerning the theoretical and methodological alternatives available to all sociologists.

Briefly, wisdom received contrasts Weber with Marx, idealism *versus* materialism, the individual actor *versus* social structure. These contrasts are all false.

Most commentators emphasise Weber's 'idealism'. They argue that he demonstrated the autonomy of ideas as social forces. Writers like Parsons and Bendix have claimed that the content of ideas, and specifically the content of religious beliefs and doctrines, have changed the course of history. When the Protestant Ethic is analysed from this point of view, reference is made to the importance of Puritan doctrines (salvation, predestination, asceticism, etc.) and their elective affinity with the Spirit of Capitalism. Almost every undergraduate student of sociology writes at some point an essay which contrasts Weber's stress on the content of religious beliefs with Marx's stress on material factors as explanations of the rise of capitalism.

Poggi does not deny these connections, but he concentrates his attention elsewhere. He is interested less in the specific doctrines described by Weber, more in how he saw Protestantism as a 'meaning–giving' force. It helped to make life meaningful for a group of people whose particular experiences, especially their changing economic experiences, were not a central moral concern of the established Church. These people were, of course, businessmen and their families, located predominantly in urban settings, and emerging as a 'burgher class'. Poggi shows how

Puritanism helped give ultimate meaning and morality to their lives. In so doing, it bolstered their sense of their own significance in the world, gave them morale and confidence to act more aggressively in society and ultimately to change it. Indeed, it is no exaggeration to say that, on this interpretation, Weber was analysing the moral basis of class consciousness.

Seen in this light there should be no radical antithesis between what Weber has to teach us and what someone like Marx has to teach us. Their insights should not be opposed to one another. They can be fused. Now it is true that neither Marx nor many of his followers have shown the slightest interest in questions of morality and morale. For them class consciousness has been a kind of behaviourist response to the stimulus of material deprivation, mediated only by the nuts and bolts of political and economic organisation. But they have neglected morality to their cost. A class which does not come to believe in its own moral destiny is incapable of great collective acts – a moral clearly relevant to the contemporary proletariat. At least one Marxist saw this clearly, however. Lucien Goldmann's *The Hidden God* (1956) analyses the reverse situation to that of Weber's burgher class. The *noblesse de la robe*, a class that is in decline in seventeenth- and eighteenth-century France, develops a tragic moral vision of its own destiny. Just as Weber analysed the confident declarations and prescriptions of the Puritan divines as representative of their class, so Goldmann analysed the tragedies of Racine and the theological paradoxes of Pascal as representative of theirs. When we have the opportunity to fuse insights like these, it is ridiculous to continue to interpret the work of Max Weber in terms of a cold war with the ghost of Marx, of idealism *versus* materialism, of capitalism *versus* socialism.

This applies also to Weber's methodological legacy. In this respect Poggi's argument, laid out on pp. 37–9 below, is even more striking. It departs radically from the individualism normally accredited to Weber. In truth Weber says that sociology is concerned with social action; that 'action' occurs where 'the acting individual attaches a subjective meaning to his behaviour'; that 'action is social in so far as its objective meaning takes account of the behaviour of others and is thereby oriented in its course'; and that therefore sociology as 'a science concerns itself with the interpretive understanding of social action'. But in this book Poggi asserts that this is not what Weber actually *does* in *The Protestant Ethic*. Here the only actor is a collective one, the burgher class. Moreover, it acts only at a time of great social flux; later it becomes thoroughly institutionalised, incapable of further action. Thus it is not the lonely individual on whom we should premise our methodology. For – I quote from p. 37 below –

> Even religious visions, necessarily the outcome of an individual's lonely confrontation with a basic existential quandary, becomes historically significant only in so far as such an individual evokes the responses of others, projects to them his or her own vision as a new ground of identity, a meaningful conception of destiny, a credible promise of justification, and in so far as, thus energised, those others reshape reality in the light of the new vision.

We should study not individual actors, but collective ones. Poggi makes clear that he prefers *The Protestant Ethic* as a guide to methodology than the first sentences of *Economy and Society*. He convinces me. It would not be the first time we prefer to follow what the founding father does rather than what he says he does. Who takes Durkheim's *Rules* as seriously as his *Elementary Forms of the Religious Life* as an exemplar of the sociological method? Perhaps Poggi can help us to recover *The Protestant Ethic* from being the ritual subject of the routine student essay and return it to its central position in the work of Max Weber and therefore in the development of sociology as a whole.

London School of Economics   MICHAEL MANN

Preface

My first intent in this book is to formulate as clearly and persuasively as possible the central argument in Max Weber's *The Protestant Ethic and the Spirit of Capitalism*. This is a very well-known text, and one which even beginning students of sociology are sometimes expected to read. It is not, however, an easy text to understand, among other reasons (I believe) because it was not written as a book, but as a lengthy, two-part essay for a major German scholarly journal of its time (1904–5), and as such it makes no special effort to render itself accessible to the reader. Its central argument is, I believe, clear and forceful. But Weber surrounded it with such a wealth of secondary arguments, qualifications, digression, he developed it with – let us say it outright – such a *show* of diverse, profound and sometimes highly esoteric learning, that its essential components and their relations are not easy to discern.

Most of the misunderstandings engendered in readers both by these peculiarities of the text and, to a lesser extent, by the intrinsic complexity of the argument itself, have been several times clarified, first by Weber himself in some complementary writings (and in emendations to the original text prepared for its re-edition in the *Gesammelte Aufsaetze zur Religionssoziologie*, 1920), then by many commentators and critics.[1] All the same, a new attempt to emphasise and rearrange what seem to me the main steps in the central argument seems warranted by the persistence of some misunderstandings, as well as by some excessively abbreviated renderings, in the secondary literature.[2]

This chief intent, to restate the central argument in Weber's text, is pursued in Chapters 4 to 6. A further intent has been to set the argument within a number of contexts relevant to an understanding of the position held by *The Protestant Ethic* in Weber's life and work. I have thus discussed the genesis of the text itself within

Weber's biography (Chapter 1), his conception of modern capitalism (Chapter 2), and his views on the genesis of modern capitalism complementary to those offered in *The Protestant Ethic* itself (Chapter 3).

Because of the frequency with which they have been raised in the secondary literature I have *not* discussed three additional, potentially relevant themes: the bearing of the other essays in the sociology of religion on the argument in *The Protestant Ethic*;[3] that hardy perennial of sociology examination papers, the issue of 'Marx *v*. Weber on the origins of capitalism'; or the historical and sociological controversy over the validity of 'the Weber thesis'. I am happy to say that the latest major entry into the literature related to that controversy – an excellent book by Gordon Marshall which came into my hands when the manuscript of my own book was already in its final version[4] – offers a most valuable discussion of the last two topics. (It also offers a restatement of Weber's own argument which, unless I delude myself, is both compatible with my own and complementary to it.)

My own Chapter 7 points to some theoretically significant features of the reconstruction of Weber's argument which precedes it. Finally, Chapter 8 outlines at somewhat greater length a further context into which that argument can be usefully set – Weber's views concerning the nature and historical destiny of the Western bourgeoisie.

As was the case with two previous books of mine, this one reflects the setting within which, over the years, I have had the opportunity to try out the ideas later committed to writing – the teaching of undergraduate courses in sociology. This is also the audience I have had primarily in mind while writing this book. I must warn such readers (and others, for that matter) that they are likely to find rather heavy going my account of Weber's conception of modern capitalism in Chapter 2; but if I hear of any complaints, I shall refer those voicing them to my chief source (Chapter 2 of *Economy and Society*), and invite them to do better themselves! No other chapter, I trust, should present comparable difficulties; at any rate, on hearing of such I shall be more willing to say *mea culpa*.

I have throughout given references to my Weberian sources (both the German editions I have used and the standard English versions) in parentheses within the text. Reference to other sources are given in the notes and references; but these are few, for I have followed my own preference, when dealing with 'classical authors', for sticking closely to their own writings, and keeping references to the secondary literature to a minimum.

I began to draft this book in the summer of 1980, in the hospitable atmosphere of the Sociology Department at the Memorial University of Newfoundland, St John's. I finished drafting it in the equally pleasant setting of the Sociology Department in the Research School of Social Sciences, Australian National University, Canberra, in the summer of 1981. The following summer, I was again at St John's, and it was there that I put the draft into its final shape. In between I have worked on this book at the University of Edinburgh. I owe special thanks for advice and encouragement to the following: Volker Meja at St John's; Jack Barbalet and John Higley at Canberra; John Holmwood and Luisa Leonini at Edinburgh. From Seattle, Guenther Roth lent valuable assistance by means of letters where approval and criticism were very skilfully and helpfully mixed. The copy-editorial assistance of Muriel Hampson and Keith Povey, and the skilful editorial advice of Michael Mann and of Steven Kennedy, are gratefully acknowledged.

G.P.

Abbreviations

Parentheses refer, in abbreviated forms, to the following sources:

1. Max Weber, *Die protestantische Ethik. I: Eine Aufsatzsammlung* (Guetersloh: Mohn, 1979). This collection, edited by Johannes Winckelmann, contains the key text: Max Weber, 'Die protestantische Ethik und der Geist des Kapitalismus', in the version prepared by Weber shortly before his death. The English translation referred to (*in italics*) is *The Protestant Ethic and the Spirit of Capitalism* (London: Allen & Unwin, 1930), and was written by Talcott Parsons. *All references not preceded by a letter are to these two texts*.
2. Max Weber, *Wirtschaft und Gesellschaft*, 5th rev. edn (Tuebingen: Mohr, 1976). Within the same parentheses the numbers *in italics* refer to the English translation, *Economy and Society*, ed. Guenther Roth and Claus Wittich (Totowa, N.J.: Bedminster, 1968). *All references to these texts are preceded by the letter W*.
3. Max Weber, *Wirtschaftsgeschichte* (Munich: Duncker & Humblot, 1923). Within the same parentheses the numbers *in italics* refer to the English translation, *General Economic History*, ed. Frank Knight (Glencoe, Illinois: Free Press, 1950). *All references to these texts are preceded by the letter A*.

Numbers preceded by the letter 'f' refer to footnotes in the Weberian texts in question.

1
The Personal Context

In this chapter I examine the circumstances in which *The Protestant Ethic and The Spirit of Capitalism* came to be written, and suggest some aspects of its theme's personal significance to its author. I raise these matters at the beginning of the discussion because by and large, in my view, it is here that belong questions pertaining to the genesis of a text – *not* because I attribute to such matters a direct and substantial bearing on the elucidation of that text, much less on the validity of its content. In fact, readers interested exclusively in the latter questions may skip this chapter entirely.

Thanks to Marianne Weber's monumental biography of her husband Max,[1] and to later biographical work which complements, qualifies, and corrects Marianne's own account,[2] we are relatively well-informed about the phase in Max Weber's life during which *The Protestant Ethic* came to be written. Incredible as it may seem to those familiar with it, this lengthy essay, which develops a complex and controversial argument and examines a huge mass of diverse material in several dead and live languages, is the product of a man who immediately previous to writing it had long suffered from an incapacitating mental illness. In this sense *The Protestant Ethic*, together with a few contemporary essays of Weber's, can be seen as the product of a spectacularly successful 'bootstraps operation', in the course of which Weber – who had early on proved himself among the most high-powered and productive scholars of his generation, and whose mind had subsequently been nearly paralysed by a mysterious malady – pulled himself out of the slough of despond, and reasserted and extended his powers in a new range of demanding and original scholarly undertakings.

In a sense, *The Protestant Ethic* is a monument to the power of love as much as to that of the intellect and the will: for throughout Max's ordeal, Marianne stood by her husband's side, giving love even when it could not be reciprocated. At the same time, Marianne may be to some extent responsible if we know less about the circumstances and the nature of Weber's illness than we might. She may have destroyed a set of notes Weber had composed to give an account of his illness to a psychiatrist; she lay a veil, in her biography, over one presumably crucial aspect of her relationship to Max, the fact that (according to other sources) their marriage was never consummated. For all this, all later accounts unavoidably remain indebted to her narrative of this painful phase of her life with Max, and draw upon her implicit or explicit suggestions as to the causes of Weber's prolonged breakdown.

Max Weber's basic psychological liability – painfully experienced throughout his life, and finding in the above illness its most acute expression – was the intensity with which he felt the urge of contradictory passions, the pressure of irreconcilable commitments. The son of a difficult marriage between ill-matched partners, he probably identified both with his intensely religious, self-sacrificing mother, and with his imperious, irascible, expansive, bon vivant father. Possessed of a moral vision that emphasised the active, responsible mastery over circumstances and events, the superiority of action over contemplation, the inescapability of risk-taking and partisanship, he was at the same time as intellectually aware as anybody has ever been that a multiplicity of standards, or end-points, can orient choice and sustain action, and that it is impossible to establish objectively the intrinsic, ultimate superiority of any such standard or end-point over others.

Early on, Weber had thought himself destined to play a leading role in German politics (his own father was at the time actively involved in Prussian political affairs). But he had later discovered himself unfit to meet some requirements of such a role, morally unable to play the game by its rules (which he knew very well). His political role had to be, at best, that of a respected commentator and critic, but one whose advice was not often heard and almost never acted upon. Passionate in his convictions, eloquent in voicing them, and uncompromising in acting upon them, he would intervene or express himself even in delicate personal matters, or those affecting the standing of other scholars, exclusively in the light of the merits of each issue as he saw them. He would thus appear at times absurdly generous toward long-time adversaries, cruelly dismissive of well-meaning critics or intending followers, or even disloyal to old associates. He often seemed to be spoiling for a fight, yet could generally see his antagonists' reasons with paralysing clarity and charity. His enduring, practised commitment to the moral greatness of Luther's defiant 'Here I stand; I can do no other; so help me God', would not preserve him from guilt whenever he felt that, in the name of his own principles, he had offended other people and *their* principles.

Let us then, with this protagonist in mind, watch a family drama unfold at Heidelberg in 1897. Since the previous year, Max Weber has held the chair of Economics at what is possibly the greatest German university, by any standards one of the world's great centres of learning. He is now thirty-three years old, has been married to Marianne for four, has his own home. The young couple have been looking forward to a visit from Max's mother, intending to offer her a much needed respite from the wearisome, often wounding co-existence with a domineering, insensitive husband. But the latter also comes to Heidelberg, and begins as a matter of course to impose his demands upon his wife, and upon the couple of whom he is the guest. In particular, he insists that his wife should remain for no longer than his own, short visit.

Already in the past Max Weber has taken his mother's side against his father, challenged the latter on family and other matters. Here, on his own terrain, his resolution not to accede to his father's claims takes the particularly dramatic form of ordering him out of his house, after an altercation in the course of which the son proclaims his growing aversion toward his father's mode of life and his treatment of his wife.

The short-run effect of this confrontation may conceivably have been cathartic for Max Weber. But as to its long-term effects, destiny plays its own hand. His father dies within a month of the incident, unreconciled with his son. Within a few weeks, a dark night of the soul descends upon the latter. Already in the past, Max's inner tensions had caused him insomnia, headaches, acute mental unease, as if to punish the compulsiveness with which he attended to his scholarly work and his duties as a professor. But now, for years on end, these and other symptoms become so severe and so hard to relieve that they are, for long periods, disabling. Although his scholarly activity is never totally discontinued for very long (it has been pointed out that even during each of the 'black years' 1897–1903 Weber continued adding to his own impressive list of publications),[3] Weber mostly finds it impossible to meet on a regular basis its normal contingencies – to confront class-room audiences; to fulfil engagements toward publishers, learned societies, correspondents; to associate with students and colleagues; to conduct research; to write. Over the next four years, outside of periods of unpredictable remission, Weber often finds himself unable to do anything but gaze vacantly out of the window, beset by guilt, frustration and despair, sheltered from any challenge, disconnected from any association, deprived of any fulfilment.

During much of the period up to 1903, the only alternative to bearing helplessly the increasing burden of Max's forced inactivity, was for the Webers to leave Heidelberg and travel, mostly abroad. Such an escape, however, could only deepen Max's embarrassment at his own condition as a spent man – at less than forty. Accordingly, he repeatedly sought to resign his Heidelberg chair; but the University demurred, and only at length, in 1903, agreed to an arrangement whereby Weber was formally relieved of those teaching responsibilities he had for years been unable to perform regularly (and which in fact he will be able to take on again only much later, at the end of his life), and given an honorary professorship. Thanks to a recent inheritance, the Webers would remain able to maintain the solid, upper-bourgeois standard of living on which I shall comment later.

Meanwhile, however, the mysterious malady was in the process of being overcome, at least in most of its acute effects. At some point in 1903, Weber felt able to resume an increasingly taxing schedule of research and other scholarly activities. He began to attend again meetings of learned societies; he undertook to be one of the three new editors of an important social science journal, the *Archiv fuer Sozialwissenschaft und Sozialpolitik*. Above all, he resumed writing.

The road to recovery was at first slow and halting; all the same, the results were spectacular. In 1903–4 Weber published four lengthy essays (the last three in the *Archiv*): two on methodological questions (a field bordering on philosophy, which Weber had never entered before, and to which he immediately made a very substantial contribution); one on an issue of legislative policy (concerning the 'fideicommissi', an arrangement concerning hereditary succession which protected, in particular, the interests of the Prussian land-owning caste), and the first half of *The Protestant Ethic*.

Biographical sources on Max Weber do not provide a fully satis-factory account of how, in particular, he went about composing *The Protestant Ethic* while still on the knife-edge between illness and recovery. There are indications[4] that he had already envisaged the essay's central thesis before his breakdown, possibly working from some suggestions made by one Heidelberg colleague and associate, the jurist Georg Jellinek. It also seems likely that during the last 'black year', 1902, his interest in the topic had been reawakened by the appearance of Werner Sombart's *Der moderne Kapitalismus*[5] (which was in turn but the latest major entry into a substantial body of literature dealing, among other things, with the relation between religious and economic aspects of Western modernisation).[6] What one cannot derive from those sources is a convincing picture of *The Protestant Ethic* being researched and written: of the extent, for instance, to which Weber relied on previously accumulated infor-mation, or undertook fresh inquiries; or of the way he conducted his writing. We do know, however, that the second part of *The Protes-tant Ethic* was partly composed during and after a lengthy, reward-ing trip the Webers made to the United States in the second half of 1904, when Max presented a paper at the Congress of Arts and Sciences organised as part of the St Louis Universal Exhibition. The trip made a significant impact on Weber's thinking on the theme of *The Protestant Ethic*, although that impact is mostly reflected in a minor companion piece, 'The Protestant Sects and the Spirit of Capitalism', about which more will be said in Chapter 6.

While we know little in detail about the genesis of *The Protestant Ethic*, it is clear that on publication it became 'an instantaneous literary success'.[7] Although until as late as 1920 (the year of Weber's premature death) it was not available in book form, but only as a two-part essay in a (presumably) decreasingly accessible journal, early on it received much acclaim and attracted much critical comment.[8] Over the next few years, Max Weber was forced several times to restate his argument against his critics; and even when the critical debate lost momentum, he returned to the topic fairly fre-quently in other writings. Indeed, in the eyes of many, he was destined to remain known, even after his death, principally as the author of *The Protestant Ethic and the Spirit of Capitalism*.

Having thus located the genesis of *The Protestant Ethic* within Max Weber's biography, let us consider briefly the *personal* background of his lifelong scholarly interest in the two phenomena at whose interface lies the topic of *The Protestant Ethic* (and of other writings of Weber's) – religion, and modern capitalism.

Germans sometimes use the expression 'die Gretchenfrage' (literally: Maggie's question) to refer to a passage in Goethe's *Faust*, where Margarete (Gretchen), in the course of a *tête-à-tête* with the enamoured Faust, asks him, 'Nun sag': Wie hast du's mit der Religion?' ('Tell me: where do you stand on religion?'). It seems suitable to ask the same question of a man who has contributed as significantly as Weber to our understanding of religious phenomena. And yet most commentators, in so far as they raise 'Maggie's question' at all, concerning Max Weber, content themselves with quoting his own statement to the effect that in religious matters he was 'unmusical'.[9]

A few students, however, not content with this clever but elusive answer, have probed further, and suggested that, whatever else it meant, 'religiously unmusical' did not mean that Weber himself was either atheistic or agnostic, nor indeed (to quote a letter by Weber himself to Toennies) 'irreligious or antireligious'. Johannes Weiss's excellent discussion of these matters[10] concludes, from a review of the evidence and the related literature, that Weber possessed a lively personal sense of 'the intimate *possibility* of a religious existence', and of the intense meaningfulness of religious experience.

What is more, Weiss provides us with a well-researched account of the evolution of Weber's personal relationship to religion – which in his case meant Christianity, and more precisely, reformed, Lutheran Christianity. He distinguishes three phases in that relationship.

In the first phase, Weber's experience of religion was shaped largely through his relationship to his mother, and to an aunt and an uncle on his mother's side (Ida and Hermann Baumgarten). These three people had in common a profound involvement in religion. However, whereas Weber's own mother embodied, in her life of piety, good works, and resigned suffering, the existential dimension of religious experience, relatively shorn of ritual and theological concerns, the Baumgartens (and particularly Hermann) were instead very interested in theological matters. (Later on, Weber was to consider this duality as a persistent contrast, within religious experience, between its lived, intensely subjective and ultimately irrational aspects, and the tendency to articulate rationally that experience, and thus unavoidably to traduce and erode those aspects) (212 f67; *233 f66*).

Although these relations made a deep impression upon the young Weber, and jointly convinced him of the significance of religious concerns, their exemplary effect in this sense was not uncontrasted. In the first place, the utterly worldy figure of his father (a man of very considerable intellectual power) exercised upon the young man an influence that often outweighed that of his intensely religious mother. Furthermore, Weber's growing acquaintance with contemporary philosophy and with biblical criticism could hardly leave untouched the dogmatic certainties of the theology dear to the Baumgartens. Slowly these experiences replaced in Weber's mind a conception of Christianity as the vision of eternal, saving truths, with a view of it that emphasised its historical role, its civilising influence. To this extent the young Weber came to share an orientation fairly widespread within cultured Protestant circles in the Germany of his youth: the so-called *Kulturprotestantismus*, which proudly asserted if not the verities of Lutheran theology then the West's cultural debt toward Reformed Christianity.

In a later phase, however, Weber came to share the concern, alive in other German Protestant circles, that by associating too closely Christianity with Western (i.e. bourgeois) culture, *Kulturprotestantismus* might further deepen the disquieting estrangement between the Church and the industrial working class. For a while Weber became associated with a wing of the so-called 'evangelic-social' movement, guided by the pastor and publicist Friedrich Naumann. Naumann's followers sought in the Gospel the moral inspiration for reforms intended to promote social justice, and thus to loosen the hold upon the proletariat of Marx-inspired (and thus in principle anti-religious) political and union organisations.

Given the declared religious inspiration of this line of political work, Weber's involvement in some of its initiatives deserves mention in our present context. However, his participation was mostly that of an expert in juridical and economic matters, and was largely inspired by Weber's personal sympathy and admiration for Naumann. In any case, without changing his appreciation of Naumann's activity and personality, Weber fairly soon came to doubt the validity of his conception of Christianity as providing the ethical inspiration for a programme of social reform. On the contrary, as he came to see the matter, the ethical message of Christianity addresses only those meaningful aspects of interpersonal relations that directly engage an individual's conscience; thus it cannot coherently be brought to bear upon class relations, whose objective, impersonal quality makes them impervious to the brotherly and charitable feelings toward one's neighbour that Christianity seeks to inspire in the faithful (95 f50; *202 f29*). In fact, Weber came to use occasionally the term 'Miserabilismus' to characterise a misguided form of political involvement motivated chiefly by a well-meaning, 'do-good' concern for the welfare of the downtrodden, disinherited strata of the population. Ethically respectable as this position might be, it has little bearing on the veritable task of politics, which – in a world divided between contending, sovereign units – necessarily consists in strengthening the power of one's national state *vis-à-vis* all others.

This view, according to Weiss, becomes further radicalised in a third phase, when Weber – very much under the influence of Tolstoy – began to see Christianity (not Christianity as an ecclesiastically embodied, historical reality, but Christianity as a radical embracement of Christ's own message of salvation) as possessing a distinctive *anti-political* orientation. As a radically other-worldly religion of love, Christianity devalues in fact *all* earthly concerns, including political, economic, aesthetic, erotic ones. Its ethical content addresses exclusively a person's inner existence, the purity of his or her intentions, the sincerity of his or her convictions.

From this standpoint it becomes ultimately irrelevant (religiously speaking) whether the world as otherwise constituted makes it easy or difficult to realise one's purely formed intentions, to act upon one's binding convictions. Once so understood, Christianity is indifferent to the growing 'disenchantment' (*Entzauberung*) of the world, and appears indeed as the only coherent way of sustaining an authentically religious attitude within a disenchanted world. As such, at the same time, Christianity enters into an intense conflict with other visions, which see one or the other worldly pursuit as imparting meaning to human existence.

We have already seen that according to Weber such conflicts among ultimate values could only be terminated subjectively, through an individual's coherent commitment to the superiority of the values he or she embraces over all others. Aware as he was that such a commitment could not be rationally grounded, Weber was determined not to allow such awareness to paralyse his own moral nerve, and personally sought to centre his own ethical vision upon the priority of political values. It would then seem that, by the same token, he could not personally respond to the appeal of Tolstoy's view of Christianity (much as he admired it and found it true to the inspiration of the Gospel); that he could not personally underwrite Christianity's inflexible devaluation of all worldly concerns (political ones foremost) as irrelevant to the pursuit of the Kingdom of God within the individual's conscience.

And yet things are somewhat more complicated. Although Weber often pointed to the struggle of many jealous Gods as a metaphorical insight into the nature of the human world,[11] he was also insistent (as we have seen) that such a struggle could and ought to be terminated by a conscious commitment to the unchallengeable superiority of one God over all others. But the locus of such a commitment, again, could only be the subjectivity of the individual's conscience, and in turn the autonomy and responsibility of such a conscience were, to him, unmistakably Christian values. Weber himself might resolutely opt, as it were, for Caesar as against God, but to be meaningful, to express and generate a coherent moral vision, that choice itself had to issue from a conscience structured as a Christian one. Luther's 'Here I stand; I can do no other; so help me God' had to be mutilated of its last clause in order to apply to the blasphemous and unChristian commitment to the German nation's power as a supreme value – but even so mutilated it remained unmistakably a Christian affirmation.

There is another sense in which Weber remained a Lutheran throughout: in his feeling that, in the modern world, a man's moral stature is measured in the first place by the extent of his identification with and mastery of his *Beruf*, his calling. Disciplined, relentless work in one's calling was to Weber the core itself of a morally dignified existence. It is poignant to think that, when in *The Protestant Ethic* Weber traced to Luther the attachment of that significance to a worldly calling, he was still groping his way out of years of much diminished activity. As his notes for the essay piled up and his drafts became more extensive, he must have felt that he was becoming whole again, recovering, in the strenuous exercise of his calling, the very ground of his being.

It remains to point out briefly the personal significance to Max Weber of *capitalism*. Or one should perhaps speak of the significance of the *bourgeoisie*: for Weber's personal attitude toward capitalism, his sense of its historical role, were probably mediated by a much more intense and explicit feeling of identification with the bourgeois class, a feeling openly proclaimed in Weber's controversial inaugural lecture at Freiburg in 1895, and frequently reasserted in his declaring himself 'a class-conscious bourgeois'.

By virtue of the professional position both of his father (a distinguished lawyer) and himself, Weber belonged in the academically trained, professional section of the German bourgeoisie. More precisely, the high social standing of the German professoriat at the time, as well as the fact that his wife possessed considerable personal means, placed Weber in the upper stratum of the bourgeoisie.

Many aspects of the several accounts we have of his personal appearance, his manners, his tastes, his style of life,[12] testify to this: for instance, the frequency and ease of the Webers' frequent travels abroad; the size and comfort of their residence at Heidelberg on the banks of the Neckar; the large amount of entertaining the Weber household routinely undertook during the many years when the Webers' circle constitued a kind of semi-permanent, high-level seminar for a large though select group of colleagues and students.

A scholar who has recently raised the matter (tabooed by other students, he suggests) of Weber's personal location within the German stratification system, and of its bearing upon his work, suggests that Weber belonged within a specific stratum which he labels '*grossbuergerlich*', and which he sees as a distinctive status group (*Stand*, estate) within a larger class unit:

> The social extraction, the life style, the forms of knowledge and codes of behaviour of the members of this group, are grounded on the distinctive features of the conduct of its existence, and on the related socialization process; and to this extent the group is configurated as an estate. It cannot, however, be considered independently of its economic basis, and thus of its position in the class system. Toward the end of the nineteenth century and at the beginning of the twentieth, at the top of the bourgeoisie there stood, in a representative position, a *grossbuergerlich* stratum, which guided and inspired the whole class, and in whose hands to a large extent, lay the class's instruments of power.[13]

Although he was outspokenly critical of many aspects of the conduct and policies of his fellow members of this stratum, by virtue of its privileged social location Max Weber undoubtedly shared many of the interests, predilections, prejudices distinctive to it; and many of these were shared in turn by that stratum's *Akademiker*-professional section, and by that other section directly vested with the ownership and upper management of the vast and flourishing capitalist sector of the German economy. Furthermore, it could be suggested that, as the holder of an Economics chair first at Freiburg, then at Heidelberg, even Weber's location within the world of learning made the nature and destiny of capitalism a topic of some personal interest to him.

Finally, both Max's and Marianne's family connections comprised several relatives who had personally been involved in establishing and running businesses, and whose success had done much to build the fortunes and the standing of the respective families. The entrepreneurial experiences of a paternal uncle of Max's, a textile manufacturer from Bielefeld, formed one basis of an important passage of *The Protestant Ethic* depicting the transition from a traditionalist to a more dynamic, modern approach to running a business (55–7; *66–8*).

Although, as I have indicated, the god of politics occupied the dominant position in Weber's personal pantheon, he had probably felt for a long time what he was to proclaim in 1920, that capitalism was 'the most fateful force of modern life' (12; *17*). Indeed, the survival of capitalism, and of an independent entrepreneurial bourgeoise, was to him a vital concern even from the standpoint of his *political* values, as a force checking the advance of bureaucratisation, maintaining an opportunity and a legitimacy for individual initiative and responsibility. In the light of those same values, and of the resultant concern of Weber's over the bourgeoisie's inability to claim its due political significance in Imperial Germany, and to shoulder the attendant responsibilities of leadership, the topic of *The Protestant Ethic* acquired a further aspect of *personal* significance to its author. For in his judgement the particular course imparted by Lutheranism to the development of Christianity in his country had denied it the experience of *ascetic* Protestantism, which in Puritan England had led to that most consequential act of political regeneration, the beheading of a monarch by his subjects in the name of distinctively political values.[14]

It was thus also in response to impulses, curiosities, concerns stemming from his own biography and social background, one may surmise, that at a crucial moment of his existence Max Weber chose as a research topic the relationship between Christianity and the rise of modern capitalism. And it was indeed in keeping with a methodological notion he was articulating at the time that a sense of 'value relevance' should orient such a choice. Coming slowly back to active existence from what must have seemed like living death to him, he raised and confronted a theme that, particularly in some of its aspects (such as the notion of *Beruf*), directly addressed his bitterest anguish, and whose treatment (as we shall see) was to convey Weber's sense of the tragic paradoxicality of historical experience.

2
The Conceptual Context

Whatever the sources of this interest in Max Weber's background and social location, undoubtedly the genesis, nature and destiny of modern capitalism held a central position among the themes of his wide-ranging scholarly production. These topics were addressed by him in all the several phases, modes and aspects of his activity: from his two earliest publications dealing with the development of early company law in medieval Italy (1889), to his last course of lectures, a 'Survey of Universal Social and Economic History' (University of Munich, Winter 1919–20), the text of which was reconstructed for publication (1923) from students' notes; from what one would call today a policy-oriented report on the organisation of the German stock market (1894–6), to an unfinished historical and comparative study, 'The City', which Weber wrote in 1911–13; from an article, '"Church" and "Sect"', published in April 1906 in the *Frankfurter Zeitung* (the first version of the companion piece to *The Protestant Ethic*, 'The Protestant Sects and the Spirit of Capitalism'), to an extensive, systematic exposition of sociological concepts concerning economic activity, in that opening section of *Economy and Society* Weber prepared for publication shortly before his death.

In fact, *The Protestant Ethic* itself may be seen as just one aspect of Weber's lifelong intellectual pursuit of that wider theme. It is a particularly significant aspect, among other things because it develops a pointed and controversial argument. However, in restating that argument, I should like to set it against the background of Weber's *conceptual* treatment of modern capitalism. This is unfortunately a rather dry topic, requiring a somewhat tortuous and involved treatment. But it must be dealt with, because in a sense it amounts to stating what *The Protestant Ethic* is all about, specifying the book's ultimate referent and that of other Weberian studies referred to above.

Within *The Protestant Ethic* itself, the concept of modern capitalism is a relatively marginal topic; that text deals with (one aspect of) the *genesis* of the modern economic order, rather than with its *nature*. Thus, in discussing the latter I shall rely almost exclusively on the conceptual introduction to the sociology of economic phenomena in the opening section of *Economy and Society*. This bringing of a later text (1919–20) to bear upon an earlier one (1904–5) is an operation implicitly authorised by Weber himself. In the last few months of his life, having decided to re-publish as a three-volume book *The Protestant Ethic* and his other essays in the sociology of religion, he preposed to the first volume an important *Vorbemerkung*. This 'Prefatory Statement' (9–26; *13–31*) contains a more diffuse conceptual portrait of modern capitalism than was already contained in the essays, and was of course written by Weber in the light of his own latest thinking on the subject, best represented in the opening section of *Economy and Society*.

The present chapter, then, complements the *Vorbemerkung*'s discussion of the modern economic order (which Weber charac-terised as a distinctive variant of capitalism) with materials from chapter 2 of *Economy and Society*, 'Basic Sociological Categories of Economising'. Here, however, Weber does not explicitly present detailed conceptual portraits of major economic systems (say, of slave economies, the medieval manorial system, or modern capitalism). Rather, he takes as his point of departure the 'economising subject', individual or collective, and details the several ways in which it can confront a whole range of contingencies and circumstances affecting, and affected by, his 'economising' activity. The resulting institutional arrangements, distilled from Weber's huge store of historical knowledge, are formulated by him with a lawyer's taste and talent for fastidiously defined, systemati-cally arrayed concepts – for example, concepts of modes of ex-change; of appropriation; of recruitment, motivation and disciplin-ing of the work-force; types of money, or of the social and technical division of labour; modalities of calculation of the outcomes of economic activity; etc.

This discussion can be brought to bear on our topic only by treat-ing it very selectively. For it covers a huge range of 'varieties of economic experience', whereas what concerns us here is *only* modern capitalism (though some of the traits by which we shall characterise it are shared with other economic systems).

Also, I shall not follow Weber and derive conceptually all features of capitalism (as well as of other economic systems) from the patterns of subjectively oriented individual action; rather, I shall adopt this approach only to convey what he meant by 'economising' (or 'economic action', as the standard English version of *Economy and Society* translates Weber's *Wirtschaften*).

'All "economic" processes and objects are so characterised by virtue of the *meaning* imparted to them – as goals, instruments, obstacles, by-products – by human agency.' In the light of this methodological principle, essential to his whole conception of sociology, Weber defines economising (*Wirtschaften*) as 'the peaceable exercise of powers of disposition' in so far as primarily intended to provide for the satisfaction of 'a desire for utilities' (W 31; *63*). This is not, alas, an utterly transparent definition, and some of its terms need clarifying.

Though the expression *Verfuegungsgewalt* is neither as infrequently used nor as execrable-sounding in German as the equivalent 'powers of disposition' is in English, this is in both languages a rather rarefied expression, which unfortunately here and elsewhere Weber uses without further definition. What he is saying, essentially, is that economising involves the manipulation of the resources at one's disposal. But he replaces 'resources' with 'powers of disposition' to keep the reader from thinking of the economising subject exclusively as one who moves about, accumulates, exchanges, works upon, *concrete, material* things; for, particularly in advanced economies, the resources sought and deployed in the economising game are also (perhaps chiefly) such abstract realities as juridically protected claims, entitlements. Thus, in particular, social relations (says Weber) constitute 'objects of economising provision' in so far as they are considered as sources of 'present or future powers of disposition over utilities'.

This latter term (*Nuetzlichkeiten*) has of course been long in use in economic theory. This is one prime reason for Weber's using it, since he intended his own sociological theory of economic phenomena as complementary to economic theory proper, which had made the notion of marginal utility the centrepiece of its formal apparatus of analysis. Another reason is again the abstractness of the term 'utility', which suitably avoids referring immediately to any concrete human wants, to 'consumption needs'.

The stipulation that, to qualify as 'economising', the exercise of a subject's powers of disposition should be 'peaceable', serves the purpose of emphasising the contrast between economising and political activity. As Weber sees the latter, it revolves essentially around the use or threat of use of force; accordingly, to him, the forceful appropriation of goods and the direct use of compulsion to extort services are political and not economic activities.

While their contrasting relations to force separate economic from political action, the boundary between the former and 'technique' (*Technik*) is posited by Weber (as by others) in the following terms. The economy has to do with the prudent choice between ends in the light of the scarcity of means; 'technique' assumes a given end, and is exclusively a matter of choice between alternative means to it (W 32–3; *66–7*). Thus a purely technical analysis of, say, certain alternative production processes, becomes an economic one when it considers the question of the respective *costs*, 'for the question of the comparative costs of the employment of various means to a given technical end points ultimately to the possibility of applying those means to different ends'.

As this definition implies, economising takes place through sequences of decisions (and their implementation): for instance, the allocation of resources between present and future uses; their assignment to the satisfaction of current wants according to their degree of urgency; the acquisition of resources through production and transportation.

In principle, such decisions may originate from and affect single individuals, grappling with the natural means and obstacles of their isolated existence. However, the social significance of economising rests on the circumstance that all sustained economic activities involve instead 'the allocation of different tasks among different individuals, and the participation of the latter in shared activities, in highly diverse combinations with the material means of production' (W 62; *114*).

This is the basic premise of Weber's effort, in the chapter of *Economy and Society* on which we are drawing, to conceptualise the enormous variety of social arrangements under which economising has taken place throughout history. As I indicated above, I shall make very selective use of his results, and convey the essential features *only* of the modern economic order as Weber saw it. I shall organise this discussion by characterising in the first place the *context* generated and presupposed by the activities of the economic *units* typical of capitalism, whose nature I shall discuss next.

The most significant characteristic of the modern economic context (as Weber analyses it) is that it comprises a *plurality* of self-contained, self-activating units, operating each on its own behalf, not in response to directives from a higher centre. (This is, incidentally, a characterisation used by many others, and whose significance has been recently stressed by Lindblom.)[1] The basic decisions mentioned above, and the related material processes (for example, the procurement of supplies and of a work-force, the technical division of labour, etc.) are the responsibility of these discrete units.

Besides carrying out internally those functions, however, such units also become tied together into the larger process by means of *exchange* relationships. Vital flows of utilities, combinations of resources, are generated by the self-regarding initiatives of the units, and by their own decisions to enter into exchanges with one another. In the modern economic order as Weber envisaged it while writing this section of *Economy and Society* in late 1919–early 1920, the prime economic function of the unitary state is not directly a matter of taking charge of the economic decisions indicated above, but that of guaranteeing the peaceable initiation and dependable performance of transactions undertaken autonomously by the units themselves.

It is on such transactions, on 'traffics', that the satisfaction of wants ultimately rests in the capitalist system (*verkehrswirtschaftliche Bedarfdeckung*). Such satisfaction is a by-product of the units' self-interested operations – as Adam Smith pointed out a long time ago. Conceptually, each act of exchange constitutes a 'compromise between the parties' interests' (W 36; 72), in the sense that its terms never entirely conform with the wishes of either party. Typically, they are settled under the pressure upon each party of the counterpart's 'contrary but complementary interests' on the one hand, and on the other of the threat posed by competitors seeking to exclude one another from the transaction by means of 'underbidding'.

In so far as the economic context, furthermore, is characterised by a *money system* (and particularly a sophisticated one, as in the case of the modern economy) the antagonist conduct of exchange partners can become oriented to *prices*. Each unit then calculates the advantages and disadvantages of varying terms of exchange over a whole range of transactions with different objects and different partners. This is because prices constitute 'going rates', stable terms of exchange, and as such, each price carries encoded within it reliable information about how all commodities relate to one another in money terms.

The further characterisation of the modern economic order as a *market system* signals that each unit's concern with its own advantage ties it directly or indirectly into all others through a complex matrix of transactions. The market is the medium of the units' mutual impacts, the locus where they all interlock. It can function in this way all the more effectively and extensively in so far as the following circumstances hold:

1.   more and more kinds of objects become marketable; *and* in the modern economic order there are markets in land, labour, capital goods, all manner of commodities, negotiable securities, money itself;

2.   the qualifications required of individuals or collective units to enter those markets as buyers or sellers are general and abstract; *and* under modern conditions an abstract, equal capacity to enter market relations attaches on an increasingly general basis to most individuals, plus an increasing number of artificial, corporate bodies;

3.   the terms of the transactions are determined exclusively by the parties' autonomous interests and by the mutual adjustments between these; *and* the modern economic system secures (largely by means of legal frameworks enforced by the state) a high degree of 'market freedom' thus understood.

The fact that at the centre of the modern economic order stands the autonomous market, where an infinite number of transactions, incessantly entered and terminated between self-interested parties, automatically and peaceably generates 'going rates', has been interpreted by many writers as implying that that order constitutes a highly fluid, relatively unstructured game, where 'any number can play', and where no unit or class of units can establish durable *power* relations with others. According to Weber, however, the context we are examining possesses a strong hierarchical structure, generates stable and visible 'constellations of powers'. The clarification of this point requires that we consider the nature of the *units* operating in that context.

The first point to be made here is that those units differ not just in their dimensions, lines of business, or organisation forms, but also and chiefly in the nature itself of their economising. Following Sombart, Weber distinguishes between two fundamental modes of economising, characterised by contrasting subjective orientations, typical meanings which the subjects attach to their own economising (W 53; *63*).

In one mode, which *Economy and Society* calls 'budgetary management' (*Haushalten*), the *point* of the economising operations is to provide for the subject's needs. When the resulting activity goes beyond a purely *ad hoc* response to acutely felt wants, and takes more rational and continuous forms, it is said to aim at securing and increasing the subject's patrimony (*Vermoegen*) and income.

In the alternative mode of economising, profit-making (*Erweb*), the provision for the subject's needs does not come directly into play: economising, rather, is a more abstract and detached matter of the subject's seeking to acquire 'new powers of disposition' over goods. Here the available stock of such powers functions as 'capital' rather than as patrimony, and the *point* of economising becomes to increase the returns of the investment of capital, of its mobilisation in gainful (though often risky) undertakings.

In the activities of any concrete economising unit, these two modes of orientation often coexist. However, it may be possible to identify the prevalent mode of orientation of a given unit, as well as to characterise a whole plurality of units, by reference to the mode of orientation dominant in their interactions. If we so characterise the modern economic order, we find that units oriented primarily or exclusively to profit-making are dominant over those oriented in their economising to the provision for needs; and this dominance imparts a distinctive hierarchical cast to the whole system. It is not a matter of there being *more* profit-making than there are budgeting units. The point is, rather, that the great majority of significant decisions affecting the nature of the goods produced, the modalities of their production, the formation and deployment of large stocks of resources, etc., are taken within units oriented to profit-making and in the light of *that* orientation. Units differently oriented must typically accept such decisions as unchallengeable constraints upon their own economising.

The profit-oriented units central to the modern economic system (whereas such units used to be marginal to previous systems) can be labelled 'enterprises' in so far as they engage in profit-making by means of 'capital accounting'. Here, at regular intervals (or, in the case of an enterprise not operating continuously, at the beginning and at the end of each profit-making venture) all the unit's assets and liabilities are evaluated in money, and the balance ascertained. 'Capital' then means the estimate in money terms of the means of profit-making available at the balancing of the books; this sum will indicate a 'profit' or a 'loss' with respect to the previous time of balancing.

Given a sophisticated money system, and a regularly functioning, 'free' market (that is one possessing to a high degree the characteristics we have listed before), such calculation can also be made *ex ante* (in advance) for the expected results of a period, or episode, of profit-making activity. The activity itself, then, can be undertaken (or otherwise) in the light of such a calculation, and if undertaken its success can be periodically controlled by comparing *ex ante* with *ex post* balances. The entities entering the calculations are based, of course, on the incurred and expected costs and prices, and thus reflect the current tendencies of the market.

Given those conditions the enterprise's operations can become oriented not so much to profit from a given operation or over a shorter period of time, as to something more abstract: profitability (*Rentabilitaet*), that is the unit's capacity to match projected with achieved levels of profit, to sustain profits, over a lengthy period of continuous activity or a whole series of profit-making ventures, by an appropriate strategy of accumulation and investment. Enterprises seeking profit through the sale of their products, in particular, can monitor their profitability in a most sophisticated manner by means of double-entry book-keeping, an accounting device whereby prevailing market prices are attached also to internal, non-market transactions between separate parts or phases of the enterprise's activities.

While the existence of 'freer' markets is a significant *external* condition if a unit is to engage in capital accounting, a vital *internal* condition is constituted by property. The typical enterprise's profit-making activities mobilise the particularly extensive and secure (because state-backed) 'powers of disposition' vested in the entrepreneur in his or her quality as the *owner* of the means of production. This allows him or her to secure the services of other individuals, who do *not* own means of production, by means of contracts of employment ('free labour'). It also normally allows him or her to integrate those services, and the workings of the material means of production, into a unified, working concern, an 'establishment' (*Betrieb*) operating continuously, with a developed internal division of labour, on the basis of the current state of technological advance.

Within modern capitalism, in fact, most capital exists, and operates, *betriebsmaessig* (W 49; *58*), that is in the form of rationally organised, continuously operating, technically unified establishments. These, furthermore, are typically involved in the production of goods – as Weber indicates obliquely by characterising modern capitalism as *gewerblich* (92 f44; *200 f23*), a somewhat archaic expression referring in his time to economic activities we would today classify as 'secondary', that is neither agricultural/extractive nor services.[2] Finally, as we have seen, such establishments employ 'free labour': that is, individuals hired on the market at a variable but calculable cost to the enterprise and responsible for their own upkeep and reproduction, provide most of the enterprise's direct inputs of muscular effort, attention, etc., in compliance with voluntarily entered contractual obligations.

These features of enterprises, which allow them to engage in profit-making in a particularly organised, continuous and (as we shall see) 'formally rational' manner, by the same token also establish their dominance over *other* kinds of units, which economise in budgetary terms. The most significant of such units are private households, which intervene in the market almost exclusively in the capacity of purchasing-and-consuming units (W 52; *97–8*). They may operate rationally in this capacity, that is maximise their marginal utilities (W 49; *92*) – but Weber rejects the view, common in economic theory (and not just in his time) that they possess ultimate control over the workings of the system as a whole. For one thing, he remarks, many consumption wants are in fact generated by enterprises through advertising (W 53; *99–100*).

The great majority of the budgetary units is constituted by the households of individuals hiring their labour to the enterprise. According to Weber, these are in a position of marked inferiority *vis-à-vis* the profit-making units, because they are 'expropriated', they lack possessions which would allow *them* to engage in profit-oriented economising, and are thus *factually compelled* to enter *formally free* labour contracts. Such contracts, futhermore, commit them to carry out their labour within the sphere of the employer's 'powers of disposition', as parts of *his* establishment, subject to his and his agents' directives. Accordingly, even their typical motivations to work will differ from their employers': the latter will be prevalently motivated by expectations of profit, and/or by their moral commitment to their calling; the former by fear of dismissal, and of its drastic consequences for their own and their family's welfare.

There are other 'budgeting' units in a system dominated (as we have seen) by profit-making ones: for instance, owners of industrial securities interested only in maximal returns. In a sense, the entrepreneurs themselves, in their capacity as heads of households with an immediate stake in the size and security of their patrimonies and incomes, economise in budgetary terms. As such, their interests are often at variance with those in long-term profitability vested in the enterprise itself. The standard practice of separating the accounts of the enterprise from those concerning its owners' private wealth, is intended to secure the functional predominance of the enterprise's distinctive interests, the conformity of its operations with the logic of profit-making rather than of budgeting (52; *98*).

Finally, there are in the modern economic system units oriented not to the profitability of long-term, productive, *betriebsmaessig* undertakings, but to other forms of profit: speculators, asset-strippers, lenders of high-risk capital, promoters of one-off ventures exploiting political connections, or aimed at quick colonial depredations.

Weber is aware of (and concerned about) the persistent, and possibly increasing, impact of such interests on the workings of the modern economic system, but on the whole he considers them marginal to it. The chapter of *Economy and Society* we are discussing pays less attention to these variants of capitalist activities than it does to an emerging, total alternative to the capitalist system. Presumably stimulated by contemporary Soviet Russian experiences in establishing and running a collectivist economy, and by the related political and theoretical debates taking place both in Russia and in other countries, Weber discusses at some length the features and the major problems of a 'unitary economy', run entirely as a gigantic budgetary system, or articulated into a number of such systems, and seeking to operate without proper prices, and perhaps without money, a market, and stably appropriated resources.

This chapter also refers occasionally, in a tone of concern, to trends current in the capitalist system: for instance, to a tendency to restrict owners' and managers' powers to discipline and dismiss workers, and (less frequently) to symptoms of increased involvement by public authorities in the running of the capitalist economy. On the whole, however, this chapter encodes into Weber's elaborate conceptual language a relatively conventional image of the modern capitalist system. As I have already indicated, he sees the state as concerned primarily to secure the system's institutional parameters through fiscal, juridical and monetary activities, rather than intervening directly into the system's functioning.

To sum up this account I shall quote a brief characterisation of modern capitalism, derived by Johannes Winckelmann from innumerable passages in *Economy and Society* (and other works of Weber's), in order to fix in the reader's mind a picture of what I have called the ultimate referent of *The Protestant Ethic*:

> This is a capitalism oriented to production, functioning through establishments, and operating on the market. It possesses the following features: 1. Fixed capital, invested in the production of goods on which depends the satisfaction of the masses' everyday needs. 2. Organisational and material means of production fully appropriated by capital owners. 3. Rational capital accounting aimed at long-run, ever-renewed profitability. 4. Orientation to opportunities (*Chancen*) open on the market. 5. Rational organisation of labour and of work discipline. 6. Rational technology.[3]

This constitutes a composite *differentia specifica* of modern capitalism as against other forms of capitalism with which the former shares, in particular, the use of money and the orientation to profit. For indeed Weber held the view (pronounced 'nonsense' by Marx) that one may legitimately and enlighteningly think of capitalism as having existed in many historical periods and many parts of the world, and saw modern capitalism (as characterised above) as, conceptually speaking, *just one* variant of that larger phenomenon. This viewpoint is explicitly stated in the *Vorbemerkung*, and is echoed throughout the chapter of *Economy and Society* on which this discussion has been based.

Among all other forms of capitalism, Weber held, modern capitalism had most successfully promoted the formal rationality of economising, by compelling economising units to operate on the basis of the most accurate calculation possible of the requirements and consequences of their activities. In these terms, modern capitalism represents an utterly unique phenomenon, superior to all other economic systems: 'In a certain sense and within certain limits, all of economic history is the history of this economic rationalism, based on calculation, which is victorious today' (A 15).[4]

Many features of the modern economic order examined above make it, in Weber's view, a uniquely suitable environment for a rational approach to economising, controlled by each unit's knowledgeable expectations about the conduct of all other units. For instance, having appropriated the material means of production, capital owners are in a position freely to recruit, train, deploy, and discipline the work-force, and thus to make predictable its performance and the related costs. 'Market freedom', given the sophistication of the modern money system, generates stable, information-laden prices, and these constitute the essential variables in the calculation of all economic inputs and outputs. By means of modern accounting techniques, the enterprise's state of economic health can be ascertained frequently and precisely, and can be insulated from the budgetary interests of its very owner. Being based on exchanges between antagonistic partners, each seeking to impose its own interests upon the others', the modern economic order necessarily entails elements of risk for each protagonist unit, but this risk itself is calculable, and this calculation can, together with many other variables, concur in forming the unit's plans.

Weber labels *formal* this understanding of rationality applicable to modern capitalism, and consisting as we have seen in the extent to which the units can form and act upon reliable calculations of the alternatives open to their economising (64; 76). He emphasises that the resultant patterns of economising in no way are also necessarily rational in a *substantive* sense, that is from the standpoint of any specific social interest or value *other than*, again, an increase in the calculability of economic action. In this latter, formal, sense, the economic system may indeed operate most rationally, and yet fail to distribute a society's worldly goods in a manner that conforms with, say, ideals of justice or equality, or that respects any particular status group's expectations of honour and security.

Weber notes that, in its mature phase, modern capitalism has satisfied to a remarkable extent the ethical demand for an improvement in the economic lot of the lower strata of the population (W 58; *108–9*); yet on a number of counts its specific vocation for formal rationality runs counter to substantive criteria. For instance, given the extent and sophistication of the price system, it is possible for consumers to maximise their marginal utilities in their budgeting choices; and in doing so they produce demand functions on which, in turn, producers can ground their own rational decisions. However, such demand functions recognise only those consumer wants backed by purchasing power (W 49; *93–4*). Thus the producers' choices oriented to such wants may well yield a supply of goods and services whose composition does *not* reflect a morally tenable conception of which human needs are more authentic and thus more deserving of satisfaction.

In general, to the very extent that they conform with formal rationality, the workings of the market ignore the ethical demand that even in their economic conduct individuals should show some degree of personal involvement with and consideration of one another, express some feeling of commonality:

> The market community, as such, is the most impersonal relationship into which human beings can enter . . . because [the market] is oriented in a specifically objective manner, oriented toward the parties' interests in the goods being exchanged, and nothing else. Where the market is allowed to give free course to these tendencies, it allows only the objective matter at hand to come into consideration, not the person. It knows no duties of brotherliness and reverence, none of the spontaneous feelings embodied in personal communities. The latter, therefore, seek to resist the tendencies inherent in the pure market community, and in turn are threatened by the interests specific to the market . . . The market's absolute impersonality is in contrast with all spontaneous forms of human relationship. (W 382–3; *636*)

According to Weber, also, the 'rational organisation of free labour' characteristic of modern capitalism heightens the calculability of the workers' performance only at a cost for the substantive rationality of the work relationship; for, sociologically speaking, the employment contract entails in fact the strict subordination of 'free labour' to the employer's domination (W 78; *138*). Thus at the very centre of the capitalist system stands, in contractual garb, an essentially coercive relation, sharply asymmetrical, and loaded with potential enmity between the parties.

We have seen that, conceptually speaking, modern capitalism constitutes *just one* variant of the very widespread and diverse phenomenon of capitalistically oriented economising. Historically speaking, however, modern capitalism has utterly unique significance, due to its distinctive rational character. It stands at the very centre not only of the economic order, but also of Western social life at large, and plays a major role in extending the hold of Western societies upon the rest of the world.

For this reason, the exploration of the conceptual features of modern capitalism (summarised in this chapter) constitutes in Weber's work only a prolegomenon to a wider investigation of its historical significance. This investigation, in turn, must perforce raise the question of the *genesis* of modern capitalism.

3
The Historical Context

Weber specifically discusses the genesis of modern capitalism in three works, addressing it in each case in a distinctive fashion.

The Protestant Ethic and the Spirit of Capitalism directly concerns itself with that topic, but seeks to establish – in essay form – only one specific aspect of it.

Economy and Society makes a much more comprehensive but less direct contribution to the topic. As we have seen (Chapter 2) while surveying a variety of institutional arrangements arising around the phenomenon of economising, formulates the conceptual material from which we have just derived a portrait of modern capitalism. Much of the rest of the book (so far as one can determine by the drafts and notes left behind upon Weber's death, edited by Marianne Weber, and subsequently re-edited by Johannes Winckelmann) was intended to explore systematically the following question: How do the institutional arrangements for economising affect, and how are they in turn affected by, those concerning other social spheres, and in particular law, religion, and politics? We can see how this question bears upon the problem of the genesis of modern capitalism if we break it down into a number of subordinate questions. For instance, what forms of religious thinking, what patterns of religious association, what fiscal and judicial arrangements, what structures of government and administration, are specifically compatible with modern capitalism, and may be said to have contributed to its development in Europe?

Finally, immediately before his death Weber dealt with the rise of modern capitalism while teaching at the University of Munich a course entitled 'Universal Economic and Social History'. The contents of this course, preserved in sets of copious and (so far as one can ascertain) accurate students' notes, have been edited posthumously as a book, *General Economic History*. In spite of its title, the course dealt mainly with forms of economic activity prevalent immediately before the advent of modern capitalism, and during the latter's early development.

By summarising the views on the genesis of modern capitalism Weber developed in *Economy and Society* and in *General Economic History* this chapter sketches the historical context within which he inscribed the argument developed in *The Protestant Ethic*, and reconstructed in the next three chapters.

As I have indicated, *Economy and Society* is relevant to our topic in the first place because it specifies some extra-economic structures favourable to the development of modern capitalism. For instance, calculation of the requirements and results of economising is, as we have seen, a central feature of modern capitalism. But calculation can only be carried out precisely and routinely, and shape a subject's rational expectations concerning his own (and others') economising, if – to use a contemporary neologism – 'numeracy' is a relatively widely shared component of a society's cultural patrimony. To that extent, the availability of relatively sophisticated arithmetical skills in the historical environment of early capitalism can be seen as one among the latter's constellation of causes (19; *24*).

Other causal components, according to the same line of reasoning, were the following: a fairly wide reservoir of technical know-how, resting in turn to some extent on scientific knowledge; a comprehensive and reliable machinery of justice, in most cases (though not all – England is an awkward exception here) run by academically trained jurists, and applying a systematised body of law; administrative structures for the keeping of order, the implementation of law, and the execution of political directives, operating largely on bureaucratic principles, and manned by trained officials.

Arguments to this effect are found not only in *Economy and Society* but also in the (contemporary) *Vorbemerkung* Weber preposed to his collected essays in the sociology of religion in 1920. *Economy and Society*, however, specifies further extra-economic conditions necessary for the genesis of modern capitalism. When presenting a typology of the modes of provision for the economic needs of political bodies, for instance, it suggests that the regular exaction of money taxes on the part of a unified, territorial system of rule is the mode most compatible with the operation of capitalistic, market-oriented firms. Another way in which Weber articulates his striking statement, in *The Protestant Ethic*, to the effect that modern capitalism had developed 'in alliance with the emergent power of the modern state' (61; 72), is by pointing to the political components of the establishment of the monetary system required for the practice of capital accounting. Congruent juridical and administrative activities of the state were also involved in establishing the degree of 'market freedom' characteristic of the growing capitalist system: for instance, in attracting within the market orbit more and more objects and subjects; in curbing or eliminating the regulation of production, prices, and consumption, by guild and community; in fostering and guaranteeing the contractual autonomy of parties to market transactions.

Weber also considers in some detail the progressive appropriation by capital owners of the means of production and the consequent reduction of workers to 'free labourers', bearing responsibility for their own reproduction, and confronting owners from a position of economic inferiority and contractually sanctioned subordination. If we consider more closely one of Weber's statements concerning the development of capitalist appropriation, we can see that a purely conceptual discussion (on the face of it) conveys in fact a great deal of historical information. Capitalism develops in so far as:

– The entrepreneur monopolises *de facto* the monetary resources of the productive establishment by means of offering advances to the workers. By thus extending credit he may assume powers of management and acquire control over the product, even where (as in handicraft and mining) the workers remain nominally the owners of the means of production.
– He appropriates the right to arrange for the disposal of the product, availing himself of his *de facto* monopoly over information concerning the market . . .
– By supplying raw materials and equipment the entrepreneur places under his own discipline even workers operating at home . . .
– The entrepreneur creates workshops without rational division of labour, by assembling into one place of work all the appropriated means of production . . .
– A final step in the capitalistic transformation of the productive establishment is constituted by the mechanisation of production

and transportation and by the adoption of capital accounting. All material means of production become ('fixed' or working) capital: the entire labour force is now constituted by 'hands'. (W 85; *147–8*)

Besides offering, in this fashion, a succinct historical account of the development of modern capitalism, *Economy and Society* also points out occasionally *why* such steps were taken, and what others followed from them. Why, for instance, does the entrepreneur manage to increase his control over resources and his command over the production process in the manner indicated? Because, according to Weber, he increases thereby the calculability of the economic performance and thus the credit-worthiness of the undertaking, hence its profitability. But, given competitive conditions, an enterprise thus made more profitable threatens less profitable ones, and compels *them* to adopt in turn those more reliable working arrangements. Thus entrepreneurial control not only increases within units, but becomes slowly generalised over the context they make up.

These forays which a primarily conceptually oriented work such as *Economy and Society* makes into the historical mode of treatment, are complemented by the discussion in *General Economic History*. However, this work contributes to our topic – the genesis of modern capitalism – somewhat less comprehensively and usefully than its title might suggest.[1]

At the time Weber taught the course on which *General Economic History* is based, he was deeply involved in redrafting the first part of *Economy and Society*. Probably as a consequence of this, although the former book has a 'narrative' structure (centred on the transition from pre-capitalistic to capitalistic economic forms), in fact it constitutes largely a survey of institutional arrangements under which (*before* and *during* that transition) were conducted such diverse economic activities as agriculture, mining, transport, credit, banking, money-coinage, manufacturing.

Under each heading the discussion ranges as much in space as over time, exploring the arrangements operated on the one hand in China, India, or Russia as against Western Europe, on the other in various parts of the latter, from England to the Netherlands to Genoa. It is as if Weber were conducting a spot-inspection of the tremendous mass of historical information from which, in the process of writing *Economy and Society*, he had 'quarried' the concepts systematically arrayed in the first part of that book. There, Weber mostly limits himself to identifying in parentheses the locale of this or that arrangement; in *General Economic History* he expands on some of these references, showing the setting within which a given arrangement had been developed, and sometimes suggesting the reasons for its success or failure. This discussion does not amount to a comprehensive account of the underlying 'story', the genesis of modern capitalism. However, various passages from *General Economic History* are put to use below in outlining such an account – which is in fact a fairly conventional one.

In the medieval West the dominant economic unit had been the *manor*, whose activities rested on the feudal relationship between the fief-holding *seigneur* and a dependant rural population, and – in terms of the basic duality of modes of economising suggested in the last chapter – were primarily 'budgetary-' oriented to the satisfaction of needs. In the early modern period, however, the typical manor began to change in the direction of capitalism, by undertaking to produce for the market, either through stock-raising or through cultivation. (Both were successfully tried in England, respectively in sheep-farming and in corn production.) In the long run, a critical effect of both phenomena was the emergence of a dispossessed rural population for which less and less employment could be found in agriculture, but which could be supported in the towns if it sold its labour on the market and thus entered the growing markets for foodstuffs and other commodities.

The significance of both the labour and the commodity markets was much increased by the strengthening of the money system, on the one hand by the increased control of territorial rulers over coinage, on the other by the inflow of precious metals from the New World into Europe. The latter phenomenon constitutes one of the three positive impulses that, according to Weber, Western overseas expansion gave to the development of capitalism. The others were, respectively, the premium that colonial rivalries among European states placed on the possession of armaments and navies (thus fostering the economic activities involved in building and provisioning both); and the development of the prototype of all later corporate aggregations of profit-seeking resources, the great colonial companies chartered in England and in the Netherlands for the exploitation of the Indies. (Weber, on the other hand, denied that the acquisition of colonial markets for home products had much significance for the early development of European capitalism.)

Although, as we have seen, the countryside had witnessed the capitalistic development of the manor, and thus 'the dissolution of the manor system' proper, the transition to modern capitalism had its chief setting in the towns; for the towns were the locale of those non-agricultural activities on which the new system was centred. They were also, however, the seat of a precapitalist form of organisation of those activities, the guild system. The latter, too, was 'dissolved' by the concurrence of a plurality of new factors. For instance, the growing demand for armaments and for other military (and naval) requirements, could not easily be met on the basis of the tradition-bound, relatively undercapitalised production practices of craftsmen. The growing significance and openness of markets undermined the arrangements whereby guilds had traditionally moderated competition among members; as a consequence, those members with greater resources and better access to markets (both as buyers and sellers) were able to reduce others to the status of wage and domestic workers. (We shall reconsider some aspects of this story in Chapter 8.)

As we have seen previously, the typical modern capitalist unit is characterised by the subordination of expropriated operatives to managerial prerogative (normally exercised by the owners or their agents) and by the co-ordination of their activities into a single establishment (*Betrieb*) whose operations are controlled through double-entry book-keeping, and whose assets are periodically verified through capital accounting. After the 'disintegration of the guilds', the organisational forms imposed by entrepreneurs on non-agricultural activities show three approximations to that conceptual target.

The first approximation is the domestic system. Here the production process is carried out chiefly in the homes of wage workers, but controlled by a 'factor' (*Verleger*) who purchases raw materials and 'puts them out' to individual workers. He may or may not provide them with their equipment, but in any case takes over the product for disposal on the market, and basically controls the workers' livelihood.

A second, transitional approximation, sees the entrepreneur gather into a workshop a plurality of workers, without tying together their activities through a technical division of labour. The fact that the entrepreneur holds within his sphere of disposition the workers' tools, not just their raw material and their product, allows him to exercise a greater degree of control over the production process than is possible under the putting-out system.

A final approximation (which does not always develop from the previous two) consists in the emergence of factories, 'where the labour discipline characteristic of the workshop is combined with technical specialisation and co-ordination and with recourse to non-human sources of power' (A 149; *162*).

In the factory system, fixed capital attains a significance it did not previously possess, and the labour force that operates it is controlled, again to an unprecedented degree, by means of organisational discipline, and with the aid of the unrelenting pressure of need and of the fear of unemployment on the workers (W 86–7; *150–51*). The chief component of fixed capital, machinery, is not so much placed at the service of the worker (as was the case with technical equipment within previous systems). Rather, the worker himself is placed at the service of the machinery (A 260; *302*). Also, while (as we have seen) the emergence of the factory system depended initially upon pre-existent scientific and technical resources marshalled by the entrepreneur, once the system becomes established it purposefully fosters further technical and scientific advance, since entrepreneurs rationalise the production process in order to make it cheaper and more calculable.

As can be seen, the progress of *industrialism* and the advance of modern *capitalism* are very closely related in this account. Weber complements it, however, with an emphasis on a phenomenon specific to modern capitalism, which he calls 'commercialisation': that is, new legal devices allow property in assets and various rights to participation in the profits of the enterprise to be represented and exchanged by means of documents. In particular, the formation and operation of joint-stock companies rests on such negotiable instruments and securities, which represent a 'means for the rational assembly of capital' – although, as Weber notes, their very existence leads to speculation, and the latter to frequent and sometimes severe crises.

Commercialisation, then, allows the formation of larger and larger aggregations of capital, which are increasingly deployed in the search for profits from the parallel growth of markets for an increasing range of industrial products. To the demand originally

generated mainly by military expansion (demand not just for armaments: uniforms are a leading product of the nascent clothing indus-
try) and by the consumption habits of court aristocracies, are added
the demand generated by the 'democratisation of luxury', and then
more widely by the rising standards of living, first of the urban
middle classes, then of wider urban strata.

The latter are increasingly composed of industrial employees,
spending their wage incomes in their capacity as consumers. Thus,
while the capitalist system has become capable of generating the
inputs of scientific and technological knowledge it demands, at the
output end it generates effective demand for its products through
the increasing dependency of the masses on wage incomes. This
ability to generate and sustain its own presuppositions allows
capitalism to play a central role in providing for the satisfaction of
the everyday needs of the whole population – a role that previous
forms of capitalism had never performed, and through which
modern capitalism supplants or subordinates all modern remnants
of non-capitalistic economic activities.

Having thus summarised Weber's account of the genesis of
modern capitalism given in *Economy and Society* and in *General
Economic History* (and in the *Vorbemerkung*), let us consider,
before reconstructing the argument in *The Protestant Ethic*, where it
fits within the above account. This requires us to consider some
aspects of Weber's general approach to the analysis of large-scale
socio-historical processes.[2]

The approach requires that we qualify the imagery, just
suggested, of the capitalist system (or of any other on-going set of
collective arrangements) as a self-standing entity with a dynamic of
its own, advancing under its own momentum. Weber never lets us
forget that any social system, no matter how solid and compelling in
its apparent facticity, ultimately rests on, indeed consists of, flows of
minded activity; and that such flows necessarily originate from
individual human beings, engage their energies, express their
strategies, convey the meanings they attach to this or that aspect of
their existence.

A system indeed can be said to exist only in so far as the mutual
activities of a number of individuals acquire and maintain a distinctive bias, which makes them predictable. The system's nature is ultimately determined by the content of that bias, by the distinctive
boundaries within which action flows, and which, in a sense, action

erects around itself. (Weber's favourite mode of sociological discourse, the conceptual elaboration of 'ideal types', is intended exactly to capture and isolate the distinctive direction of a given bias. Accordingly the basic intuition behind his elaborate, systematic typologies is that, when all is said and done, there are *only so many* ways of, for instance, legitimising authority, accounting theologically for evil, or allocating social power among groups.)

The operation of the modern capitalist system, then, should be seen as the outcome of a myriad of interlacing, mutually referring human acts. At bottom, capitalism only exists in so far as a multitude of individuals orient in certain distinctive ways their economic activities. Heads of firms seek to improve their profit margins, and thus try to predict the demand for their commodities and to monitor their competitors' strategies. Production managers devise innovations in the firm's technical operations; managers seek to maximise output per unit of input, and to this end control as closely as possible the flow of materials, each expenditure of human and mechanical energy; operatives comply promptly with managerial directives, and use tools competently and raw materials sparingly. The same keen, sober-minded approach to economising applies to consumers, who seek to maximise the marginal utility of their expenditures, and to that extent generate information-laden prices, to which firms orient their strategies (W 49; *93*).

This view of the capitalist system as the resultant of innumerable flows of minded activity of individuals, raises the problem of the subjective springs, the *motivation* of such activity. Why do actors typically conduct themselves in a manner indicated? What meaningful considerations sustain the attention required to scrutinise continuously one's economic conditions and means of action, the effort required to revise one's lines of conduct accordingly?

Weber's answer to these questions shows that the imagery of capitalism as a self-sustaining system does contain some valid insights; for he sees the activities that generate the system as themselves in a sense generated by it. According to him, each actor's economic conduct is largely motivated by the subjectively perceived *necessity* of complying with the system's demands. True, at the top, the entrepreneur's compliance is proximately motivated by the aspiration to gain the system's rewards in the form of profits (12–13; *17*), whereas at the bottom the workers' compliance arises chiefly from fear of the system's decisive penalty, unemployment, and of the attendant disastrous consequences for oneself and one's family. Yet, however different, these are but two different modalities of the same constraint to adapt oneself to the system's logic, embodied in competition. By allocating both its rewards and its penalties according to that logic, the system automatically engenders motivations and modes of conduct congruent with itself; it selects individuals capable of prospering or surviving in it, and marginalises or eliminates those not so capable. By the very logic of its operation, then, modern capitalism generates in actors the subjective orientations it thrives on, and to that extent constitutes indeed a self-sustaining, going concern (45; *54–5*).

However, capitalism's ability to generate its own presuppositions (which we have already acknowledged in its capacity to generate the inputs of scientific and technological information it needs, and to generate effective demand by means of wage employment) is a property it acquires only once it has become the *dominant* economic system, once the search for profits and the 'cash nexus' of the employment relation have become by far the most significant sources of income. However, that property cannot be called upon to account for the processes whereby the system itself *arose* and *established itself* at the centre of a society's economy. In other terms, the problem of the system's *genesis* as against that of its *functioning* requires a distinctive answer, itself in keeping with Weber's constant emphasis upon the subjective, meaningful components of the socio-historical process (53; *63*).

In the first part of this chapter, we have derived some insights into the genesis of modern capitalism from its conceptual treatment in *Economy and Society*. Those insights have their own limitations. On the one hand, they point to some environing, extra-economic conditions capitalism needed in order to develop; on the other, they suggest some requirements of its economic characteristics, such as, for instance, the expropriation of subaltern social groups. Both lines of analysis, that *via* 'environing conditions', and that *via* 'prerequisites', first postulate the system and then argue back to its presuppositions, respectively external and internal to it. To account satisfactorily for the system's genesis they must be complemented by a consideration of the *collective actor* who undertook to make use of the favourable environing conditions and implemented the prerequisites of the new system's essential traits (45–6; *55–6*)

To justify this statement we must consider in general terms the relationship between 'system' and 'actor'. If *systems in being* should be seen as sets of constraints that individuals adapt to and act upon, then the *making of systems* is a matter of laying down new constraints. And it is a general principle of Weber's approach (a principle assumed and occasionally affirmed, rather than explicitly articulated, in *The Protestant Ethic*) that only collective actors can exercise leverage upon existing constraints, modify their bias, replace them. Even such actors, of course, cannot fashion new constraints at will. They exercise their leverage within broad bounds, the nature of which it is (again) the task of ideal-type construction to identify.

Thus, the engine of the historical process (in so far as it lends itself to sociological analysis) is the pressure exercised by groups upon the existent constraints on modes of human feeling and experience, a pressure mostly exercised in the name of suppressed interests, heretical values, unmobilised resources, unsanctioned visions, previously untested devices (46; 55). Even religious visions, necessarily the outcome of an individual's lonely confrontation with a basic existential quandary, become historically significant only in so far as such an individual evokes the response of others, projects to them his or her own vision as a new ground of identity, a meaningful conception of destiny, a credible promise of justification, and in so far as, thus energised, those others reshape reality in the light of the new vision.

If applied to the genesis of modern capitalism, this elementary model of explanation suggests that a critical part in that genesis must have been played by a plurality of people who could not satisfactorily pursue their own interests within the pre-existent economic system, and who together developed enough momentum to displace the system's boundaries and lay down new ones, conducive to their own interests. In other terms, the problem of the system's genesis cannot be solved purely by pointing to the environment of that genesis (the mode of explanation summarised by Weber in the *Vorbemerkung*). Its solution requires that we identify a *body of personnel* which, acting upon interests of its own and mobilising distinctive resources, saw the new opportunities present in that environment, and defeated the opposition to their realisation.

Now, the Weberian arguments on the nature and genesis of capitalism – as well as (it might be said) plain common sense – leave little doubt as to the identity of the relevant collective actor. This was the early capitalist entrepreneurship – a fairly large and diverse body of men who, starting broadly from the middle of the seventeenth century, initiated various commercial and productive innovations, culminating in industrialisation, which revolutionised the European economy.

Commonsensical as this position is, it was not utterly uncontroversial at the time Weber wrote *The Protestant Ethic*. In the text he makes several references (e.g. 48; *57–8*) to an alternative position, according to which the historical task in question had been carried out chiefly by a few 'economic supermen' of the Renaissance period: highly innovative enterprisers, founders of powerful banking and commercial dynasties, such as the Medici, the Fugger, the Welsers. Weber held, however, that such figures embodied a form of capitalism different from modern capitalism, and that the latter's genesis had as its protagonist a larger group of rather less flamboyant people (46; 55).

It might be noted that the notion itself of a *collective actor* is not unproblematical for an author such as Weber, who, as we have seen, insisted on positing individuals as ultimately the only active entities in the socio-historical process. On this assumption, a number of discrete individuals can be said to constitute a collective actor only in so far as they can plausibly be seen as oriented and propelled by shared interests.

Thus it makes sense to speak (as we have done) of a 'body of personnel' as the collective protagonist of an historical transformation only if a distinctive set of interests can be, if not empirically reconnoitred within the minds of single individuals, then plausibly imputed to them on the basis of the situation common to them, and of the materials and intellectual resources available in that situation, or which the individuals themselves develop in the course of their activities. Thus, we can speak of the early capitalist entrepreneurship as a collective actor only if we can plausibly construe its 'makings', locate a distinctive set of circumstances, interests, perspectives they shared.

If we now reconsider briefly the account of the genesis of modern capitalism summarised in the first part of this chapter, in the light of a broad distinction between economic and extra-economic factors, we find that the latter have appeared in the account mainly as aspects of the *environment* of the process in question; that, in particular, some peculiar legal, political, intellectual structures were considered by Weber as necessary conditions for the rise of modern capitalism. On the other hand, in dealing (explicitly or implicitly) with the collective protagonist of the genesis of modern capitalism, we have so far emphasised economic determinants. In so far as we have considered them at all, we have construed the early entrepreneurs' strategies as resulting from their interest in accumulating capital and increasing profits, by means of the financial and productive resources under their command and (increasingly) under the stimulus of competition.

However, the chief assumption behind Weber's argument in *The Protestant Ethic* is that this construction of the collective identity of the early capitalist entrepreneurship is too narrow; that that identity possessed essential extra-economic 'makings'; that the entrepreneurs' economic activities themselves were oriented, given momentum, *also* by a moral vision, an ethical code, a meaningful conception of life and conduct, a 'spirit'.[3]

On this assumption, *The Protestant Ethic and the Spirit of Capitalism* builds an argument that falls neatly into two parts. The first construes the 'spirit of capitalism' as the critical extra-economic component of early capitalist entrepreneurship; the second locates (chiefly) in Calvinism the religious underpinnings of that spirit. In the next three chapters, we shall reconstruct this argument.

4
The Argument, I: The Spirit of Capitalism

'Spirit of capitalism' is the label (not of his own devising) that Weber attached to his own construct of the distinctive normative pattern of conduct of the early capitalist entrepreneurs. In developing that construct he was guided by the criterion of 'adequacy': that is, the pattern had to be congruent with the peculiar institutional features of modern capitalism, responsive to the specific burdens and opportunities that activity presented for the economising subject, at a time when most economic activities were *not* conducted in the modern capitalist mode (54; *64*).

The first and possibly most vital feature of the spirit of capitalism is that it invested economising itself with high moral significance. That is, the entrepreneur (and to lesser extent this might have applied also to other economising subjects, including workers) engages in capitalistic economising not purely as a matter of expediency, of constrained adaptation to the mundane necessity of making a living, but in the expectation that such activity would test his inner resources as an agent, as a person in charge of his own existence, and affirm his human worth.

To paraphrase a striking saying of Durkheim's about religion, for the typical early entrepreneur *l'économie, c'est de la vie sérieuse*: the tasks of the enterprise are performed with an earnestness of purpose that places them at the very centre of the subject's life, endows them with intrinsic dignity. There is nothing degrading about them, nothing demeaning about the attention to minutiae they require, nothing requiring apology in the style they impart to the entrepreneur's whole existence. He indeed expects his work to shape his very identity, to mobilise and develop his most personal qualities. In a word, the spirit of capitalism enjoins the entrepreneur to consider his economic activity as a calling (*Beruf*) (63; *74–5*).

But the concept of calling is not applicable only to the gainful activities performed on the market (as the entrepreneur's are): it can be used to characterise such varied pursuits as those of the priest, the soldier, the physician or the bureaucrat. Now, traditionally in these contexts the demanding and ennobling nature of the respective activities was affirmed by vesting in the practitioner claims to income (the priest's benefice or living, the physician's or the lawyer's honorarium, the bureaucrat's stipend) institutionally different from direct monetary gain from the sale of goods or the performance of services. However, in the case of the entrepreneur a concern with monetary acquisition as such was unmistakably and directly at the centre of his calling. If it is about anything, being an entrepreneur is about making money; his activity is obviously and primarily intended to benefit him, possibly (or unavoidably?) at other people's expense.

Thus, to be credible as a proper calling, entrepreneurship needed, as it were, to sublimate its intrinsic concern with monetary gain, by orienting it and disciplining in distinctive ways, which the spirit of capitalism enjoined upon the individual entrepreneur (42–5; *51–5*). On the one hand, his approach to monetary gain was markedly different from a manifestation of the sordid passion of greed (47; *56*), in that such gain was not to be put to use primarily to satisfy the urges of gluttony, sloth, lust, intemperance, ostentation, luxury, and self-indulgent bodily comfort; rather, it was to be saved, accumulated. On the other hand, the resulting frugality of the entrepreneur's way of life could not be mistaken for the sheer retentiveness of the miser; for the resources accumulated would be continuously employed in the enterprise, as a means to future gain (to be treated, again, in the same manner).

One might characterise this attitude toward money and gain as marked by 'non-immediacy': for money is not to be immediately spent for pleasure or display, nor to be immediately enjoyed as a hoard, as an intrinsically rewarding, gloated-over possession. Rather, it is to be treated, as we have seen, as a means to future returns.

In turn, the subjective cast of the expectation of such returns can again be contrasted with two opposing patterns. On the one hand, the treatment of money as capital involves an element of risk, and to that extent differs from the rentier's expectation that his past acquisitions (or, indeed, his inherited patrimony) will automatically and safely work for him. On the other hand, the risk involved is not a matter of hazard or of venturesome speculation, to be realised or exploded in one fell blow; it is a calculated and controlled risk – and the chief means to its control is the entrepreneur's own activity. The entrepreneur must himself *work* to make his money work for him. His attitude toward money can be best characterised as one of stewardship: money is only potentially useful, and the realisation of that potentiality depends on sustained, careful, responsible activity. Such an attitude can be best maintained when the monetary resources are seen as vested not so much in the entrepreneur himself, as in his business, conceived as a distinctive entity, with interests and a logic of operation of its own.

This conception, in turn, is kept alive in the entrepreneur's mind by some objective features of the capitalist business. In the first place, as we have seen, book-keeping devices separate the business's accounts from those of the entrepreneur's or his family's wealth. In the second place, the business operates often on loaned funds, and must satisfy the creditors' claim to a return. In the third place, the business typically finds objective embodiment in an establishment (*Betrieb*), an assemblage of diverse resources. At any given time only a small part of the entrepreneur's assets will be available as cash: the majority are constituted by productive equipment, raw materials, a flow of products at various stages of realisation, a stock of finished products awaiting disposal on the market, an invisible but crucial store of market information and of suppliers' and customers' good-will. What holds the assemblage together as an establishment is, on the one hand, the flow of live labour from employees, on the other the entrepreneur's organising activity, his ability to activate and direct the performance of live labour itself by means of remuneration and by the exercise of discipline.

But in so far as the establishment is a set of components sharing a functional destination to produce a return on capital under the entrepreneur's control (and at his risk), each of these components must be seen as a manipulable variable, and the entrepreneur is expected continuously to survey and assess a whole range of possible combinations of those components, in order to realise the combination likely to yield the best return. Indeed, he must consider no given combination as ultimately fixed; he must be willing to tinker, however marginally, with all established arrangements, technical and organisational. Thus, the spirit of capitalism imposes upon the entrepreneur an open-ended, open-minded attitude, disposes him continuously to make choices, introduce innovations, with the assistance of accounting devices that attach hypothetical costs and yields to any given combination.

For this reason (and one may see in this a further manifestation of what I have called 'non-immediacy') the entrepreneur's identification with his calling is not allowed to take the form of a commitment to any narrowly profiled, traditionally sanctioned set of practices (his own or his employees'). All practices are adopted (and employees are made to follow them) provisionally, and continuously tested for their respective returns. Even the expected rate of profit is to be considered a variable, and in order to maximise it the entrepreneur must be willing to disengage himself from a given market or a given line of business.

If we review these features of the mental and moral habitus the spirit of capitalism fashions in the entrepreneur, we may see them as involving a peculiar attitude toward time. On the one hand the entrepreneur is unmistakably oriented toward the future, as is shown negatively by his abstention from present consumption and ostentation and by the willingness to ignore and violate tradition, and positively by his expectation of a long-run return from investment. On the other hand, there is no question of simply casting one's bread upon the waters of time. There *will* be returns only in so far as the 'time of the enterprise' constitutes a self-repeating cycle of continuous activity whereby capital advances toward its expansion, each single moment bearing both a promise of gain and a threat of loss. Thus the entrepreneur's own time must be a continuum of activity, a self-repeating sequence of controlled and calculated acts of risk-taking. He can only minimise the threat and maximise the promise held within time's flow, then, by imposing upon himself a methodical attitude, accepting the burden of relentlessly monitoring the environment, verifying his assets, adjusting their composition.

But since (as the concept of 'calling' implies) the spirit of capitalism centres the entrepreneur's whole existence around his business, unavoidably his attitude toward time comes to shape also his attitude toward other human beings – primarily of course (though not exclusively) toward his business associates and employees. Here, the parallel to the renunciation of immediate gratification from gain (which would consume the results of past activity instead of turning them into the instruments of future activity) is a reduction of the immediate emotional content of one's association with partners and customers, a 'cooling', one might say, of one's relations with customers and employees. The parallel to the watchful and active expectation of future gain is the careful building of trust between oneself and one's creditors and customers, and the specification of reciprocal duties and rights *vis-à-vis* workers by means of the employment contract.

In the latter context, however, as in the relations with competitors on the market, there is an unavoidable element of conflict. Should this conflict become open and explosive, it would become impossible to entertain reliable expectations about the outcome of one's business activity. But the *form* of such conflict is controlled by a body of public rules; and the *content* of the conflict's resolutions is objectively dictated by the 'going rates' on different markets (for labour, for commodities, for credit and securities), and by the necessity of adjusting to those if the enterprise is to stay in business.

As the steward of the firm's resources, the entrepreneur cannot afford to respect his employee's attachment to this or that productive practice, or their expectation of a given mode and level of remuneration; he must impose on them the innovations that in turn the market imposes on him. Thus the prevalent features of the network of social relations and of the flow of interactions occasioned by the practice of entrepreneurship are impersonality and objectivity. The entrepreneur's involvements with other human beings must be kept from interfering with the requirements of capital's realisation and expansion, and to that end must be made shallower, more specialised, less durable, more open to change than they might otherwise be. Ideally the entrepreneur must adopt toward all others a detached attitude, deal with them even-handedly, matter-of-factly, correctly. Only in this way can he increase his own self-control and his sense of responsibility.

Clearly, then, no deeply felt commonalities shape the social context of the entrepreneur's activities. As we have seen, he must behave even to his closer associates in a detached manner. His main tie to his employees is the cash nexus, and they are likely to resent his exercise of managerial prerogatives. On the market, his relations to his competitors are in the nature of a muted conflict. In sum, in so far as he practises his calling in accordance with the spirit of capitalism, the entrepreneur is normally prevented from entering with his fellow humans into deeply solidary relations, and is unavoidably thrown back upon himself, placed into a moral posture which we can characterise as individualistic. Yet he is not allowed to become overly absorbed into, preoccupied with, himself; the shallowness of his social relations is compensated instead by the depth of his active and responsible involvement in something outside himself, by his 'surrender to the matter' (59; 69) of the firm's welfare. His existence revolves around an objective concern, which unceasingly demands his devotion and offers itself as the test of his worth.

All these traits of the spirit of capitalism can be seen as aspects of one central injunction – that the entrepreneur should master his situation and control the outcome of his activity by acting *rationally*. Rationality is enjoined upon him in contrast with traditionalism, with the slavish or unreflected adherence to past practices and arrangements. Rationality, as against the impulse of emotion, is to guide his relation to associates and employees. He is expected to arrange and rearrange his productive resources, ordain the flow of live labour under his command, by rationally assessing his circumstances and the opportunities they offer. He is to be guided by rationality both in considering longer stretches of future time than he could encompass if impelled by immediate need or greed, and in making each of the choices with which individual moments continually confront him. The attachment of money-values to all his assets, from the smallest item in the firm's inventory to the good-will of the last customer, allows him to employ the most pliable and sophisticated aid to rational choice, mathematical calculation. Arbitrium, tradition, emotionality – all alternatives to rationality are expunged from the range of considerations motivating and guiding the entrepreneur's conduct, or at any rate their impact is reduced as much as possible. In so far as he abides by the spirit of capitalism, then, the entrepreneur commits himself to the strenuous practice of rationality.

By its very nature, however, that practice requires a reference to a goal, a fixed target against which to test the effectiveness of different combinations of means. The spirit of capitalism (as, indeed, the nature of modern capitalism itself) clearly establishes the increase of capital as this ultimate point of reference. In a sense this goal itself reflects the orientation to rationality, and in that sense the goal is, as it were, homogenous with the rational practices aimed at it. It is objective; it is quantitative; it is mobile, since each capital increment is to lead to further increments.

In another sense, however, capital expansion, while providing a rational standard for all entrepreneurial practices, is *not* itself rational in nature (268 f273; *276 f79*). In fact, it cannot be, exactly because it is postulated as the ultimate target of rational enterprising, and as such cannot itself be the object of rational justification (44; *54*). Indeed, how can one possibly justify rationally an acquisitive activity that systematically prohibits (or indefinitely postpones) its protagonist's direct enjoyment of the fruits of his own success, in the interest of accumulation? How can possible be called ultimately rational a mode of activity that requires the individual to treat his associates detachedly and impersonally, where the terms of all interpersonal relations have only provisional validity, since they are continually modified by the market's changing circumstances? (59–60; *70–2*).

In the light of these questions, the rationality the spirit of capitalism enjoins upon the entrepreneur appears partial and potentially contradictory, for it is made to serve a goal which is in turn irrational or at least a-rational. Yet that goal (capital expansion) is unmistakably the lodestar of the entrepreneur's calling, and is expected to be the very centre of his existence (59; *70*). We are thus brought back to the first remark we made about the spirit of capitalism: its point is to attribute moral significance to entrepreneurial activity, not simply to supply a set of pragmatic rules for the pursuit of an utterly utilitarian end (44; *53–4*). The spirit of capitalism is intended (also) to lend *meaning* to the existence of those committed to it. As such, according to Weber, it has and can only have an irrational or a-rational option at its core (268 f273; *276 f79*). It must constitute, for those embracing it, an existential wager.

In this sense, then, the spirit of capitalism is indeed a *spirit*, an Ethos, a vision capable of imparting meaning only to the existence of those untroubled by its lack of further rational justification (42; *51*). What differentiates it most sharply from other such visions is possibly its unique dynamism: the relentless drive it inspires in the individual fully committed to it. Such an individual is peculiarly (to phrase this point with the young Marx) 'ein gespanntes Wesen', a tensed-up being, who in complying with that vision both expresses and releases the tension the vision itself generates.

The above is my own restatement of the notion of 'spirit of capitalism' presented by Weber in *The Protestant Ethic*. Before moving on in the next chapter to the theme of the religious determinants of that spirit, I should like to raise two questions about the logical status of the argument developed in this chapter.

First, did Weber simply intend to put forward a credible construct of the spirit of capitalism, or did he also intend to *prove* that that spirit had dwelled in the minds of the early capitalist entrepreneurs? It seems to me that Weber thought the latter task impossible, and did not pursue it. It may seem otherwise, because his own statement of the spirit's nature consists largely in comments upon extensive passages from Benjamin Franklin's *Necessary Hints to Those Who Would Be Rich* and *Advice to a Young Tradesman* (40–47; *48–58*). But I think that Weber used those texts to characterise the content of the spirit of capitalism, *not* to establish its existence in the minds of entrepreneurs. In fact, for Weber (as I read him) those passages were only an expository device, proving (at best) that the capitalist spirit dwelled in Franklin's own mind, but otherwise useful as textual support to his own imaginative reconstruction of the 'mind set' of the early capitalist entrepreneurs (40; *48*). He believes, and invites his readers to believe, that the latter actually entertained ideas similar in content to those making up that construct. But one can share that belief (as I personally do) and still see *The Protestant Ethic* as suggesting its plausibility, rather than arguing a proof.

The second question is a more arduous one. Suppose we accept, on whatever grounds, that the spirit of capitalism was indeed actively present (as a set of consciously entertained and 'consulted' ideas) in the minds of the typical early capitalist entrepreneur. Does

The Protestant Ethic prove, then, that this made a significant difference to the larger story; that the spirit of capitalism was an essential
(though of course not sufficient) condition for the genesis of modern
capitalism?

I would answer this question with a strongly qualified 'no'. 'No',
because, again, I believe it impossible to offer conclusive proof to
that effect (or to the contrary effect, for that matter): 'strongly
qualified', because Weber, while himself (probably) convinced of
that impossibility, did nevertheless make an impressive case for
seeing the spirit of capitalism as one of the causes of the development of modern capitalism. In the balance of this chapter I shall
review some of his arguments to this effect.

A strong methodological objection to attributing any independent causal significance to the spirit of capitalism may be phrased as
follows: Weber determines the content of that spirit on the assumption that it must be 'adequate to', functionally congruent with, the
institutional features of modern capitalism; by the same token,
however, he renders unacceptable any strong claim that that spirit
was among the causes of capitalism. For, if you infer from *A* the
existence and the nature of *B*, you cannot then go and make a strong
case for *B* causing *A*. In fact, once the capitalist spirit is construed on
the assumption of its congruence with the economic structures built
and operated by the early entrepreneurs, one might if anything feel
justified in considering the ideas making up that spirit as an ideological expression of, an adaptation to, the material interests inherent
in those structures. As such, those ideas would possess no independent significance and certainly not the significance of causes of those
structures.

Without explicitiy raising this objection, Weber suggests one
possible response to it. While it is the case that (as I read him) he
derives the spirit of capitalism from its institutional structures, he
states repeatedly that the two do not always and necessarily occur
together. In certain historical circumstances we observe capitalism's
distinctive 'form' (which in this context means its institutional
structure, its visible mode of operation), whereas the individuals
operating enterprises do not appear motivated by anything like the
capitalist spirit; in other circumstances we find the spirit affirmed
and acted upon ahead of and in the absence of the congruent

institutional structures of economic activity. (Weber gives as one example of this second phenomenon the case of Franklin himself, articulating the capitalist spirit in a precapitalistic economic environment) (46; *55*).

This distinction between 'form' and 'spirit' (e.g. 47, 54; *56, 64*), and Weber's insistence on the possibility of their disjunction, address the above objection in two senses. In the first place, if 'form' and 'spirit' of capitalism may occur independently of one another, then, in spite of the methodological device of deriving the latter from the former, the relationship between the two is a contingent one; and in particular, if the spirit is sometimes found ahead of the form, then it cannot be considered simply and generally an adaptation to or a product of it. In the second place, if form and spirit of capitalism can occur historically in disjunction from one another, then one may attach particular significance to those instances where they do occur together. The emergence of early capitalist entrepreneurship may be considered one such phenomenon: here, a relatively large body of men engaged in capitalist practice *and* shaped their own existence in accordance with the capitalist spirit (92 f44; *200 f23*). It was (it might be suggested) this very conjunction that allowed such men to exercise tremendous leverage on the course of history by first establishing capitalism as a going concern.

I shall break down into two steps a further argument of Weber's suggesting (though, again, not proving) the distinctive historical efficacy of the spirit of capitalism. First step: The spirit of capitalism is a unique phenomenon, not to be mistaken for just another ideological justification of sheer greed, a fancy disguise of the *auri sacra fames*, of the execrable hunger for gold. It does not simply sanction acquisitiveness or prescribe techniques of self-enrichment. Rather, it constitutes a moral habitus, which (as we have seen) burdens the possessor of money with a steward's obligation toward his own possessions.

Second step: *Nothing can be so different and yet make no difference.* This is my own phrasing of a point Weber makes in the related context of his comments upon the historical novelty of Luther's concept of *Beruf*: 'Astonishingly, there are students according to whom a development of such novelty may simply leave no mark upon men's *conduct*. I must confess that I do not understand this at all.' (108 f61; *212 f9*).

One may see *The Protestant Ethic* as making a (strong?) case for the independent causal significance of the capitalist spirit, furthermore, by considering its argument as an application of a wider theoretical position, which I have already stated in Chapter 3. According to this position, large-scale historical innovation is always the product of groups; groups exist in so far as 'interests, material and ideal' are shared among pluralities of individuals; and ideas, in particular, 'like switchmen, determine the direction in which the dynamics of interests propel human action'.[1] If we treat this often-quoted statement of Weber's as an *otherwise validated theorem*, then of course one may subsume *The Protestant Ethic*'s argument under it, consider it as derived from it. But it is important to consider the liabilities of this intellectual operation, which presume that we are starting *from* a previously established generalisation; whereas it has been claimed (by Weber and others) that *The Protestant Ethic* itself constitutes a major advance *toward* that generalisation. All the same, speaking entirely for myself, one reason why I find *The Protestant Ethic* convincing is its accord with a more general explanatory principle which strikes me as valid.

Finally, it might be said that Weber approaches more rigorously the task of proving the causal significance of the capitalist spirit when he complemented *The Protestant Ethic* with a series of massive studies of 'the economic ethic of the world religions' – chiefly Confucianism, Hinduism, Buddhism, and ancient Judaism.[2] Here he sought to establish that in the respective civilisations, in spite of several conditions favourable to the development of something similar to modern capitalism, no such development had taken place, among other reasons *because* those civilisations possessed no ethical understanding of entrepreneurial activity closely similar to the spirit of capitalism. Now, however otherwise impressive this strategy of explanation may be, its bearing on the question of that spirit's causal role in the genesis of modern capitalism in the West seems to me rather indirect. For in those essays Weber largely presupposes as proven the link between that spirit and Calvinism, and attributes the failure of those civilisations to promote the development of capitalism largely to the inexistence within them of a body of religious thinking akin to Calvinism.

To sum up, I do not see *The Protestant Ethic* (or other works of Weber's) as offering conclusive arguments to the effect that the spirit of capitalism made a decisive (though partial) difference to the development of modern capitalism. But the cumulative weight of his several and variously persuasive arguments to that effect seems to me considerable.

5
The Argument, II: The Search for Religious Determinants

We turn now to the central problem in *The Protestant Ethic*, enunciated in its title: the search for the religious determinants of the spirit of capitalism. This should be seen as just one aspect of the wider problem of the causal makings of that spirit – it being a methodological axiom, to Weber, that all major social phenomena have behind them a matrix of multiple determinants (77; *91*). This axiom, however, does not place out of court an analysis focused on a single cause (or class of causes), even at the risk of what one may call a provisional exaggeration of its significance.

As to Weber's decision to focus on *religious* determinants, some of the considerations in Chapter 1 of this book concerning his own religious attitudes may be relevant here – in particular the emphasis, characteristic of the *Kulturprotestantismus* with which at one point the young Weber had become associated, upon the cultural and civilisational legacy of the Reformation. But that association was a past matter by the time Weber wrote *The Protestant Ethic*, and the above decision lends itself to understanding in the light of less personal considerations.

One important consideration, I believe, concerns Weber's keen feeling for historical paradox. For, on the face of it, the spirit of capitalism enjoins upon the subject a peculiarly irreligious or a-religious attitude toward existence. Not only does it make the continuous increase of one's capital into the self-justifying goal of one's economic activity; it also places that activity (as a 'calling') at the very centre of the subject's whole life. The resulting, pervasive attitudes of matter-of-factness, impersonality, antitraditionalism, individualism, seem likely to generate in the subject a thoroughly secular orientation, preventing him from becoming seriously concerned with his other-worldly fate, or from cultivating the traditional Christian virtues of brotherliness, charitableness, acceptance of one's estate in life.

Indeed, to Weber (as to Marx) the capitalist system appears as the main force promoting the universal secularisation of existence (the 'disenchantment of the world', in an expression Weber derived from Schiller). But in so far as (Weber claims) the capitalist spirit has contributed to the instauration of that system, does this not make it implausible that such spirit should have religious causes? It would seem that religion (Christianity, at any rate) can at best have assisted *by default* in the genesis of the chillingly secular posture to which the spirit of capitalism attributes ethical value; that one of the causes engendering that spirit must have been a religious vacuum, a diffuse attitude of religious indifference, rather than a religious vision imparting a positive sanction to that spirit.

Yet, paradoxical relations between events are, according to Weber, the very stuff of history; and on this count alone, looking for the religious determinants of the capitalist spirit does not amount to such a hopeless wild-goose chase after all. More important, there are positive reasons for undertaking such a search (61;72).

First, as Weber says, religion has ever been among the most significant forces shaping the development of ethical views (21; 27). Exacting and coherent designs for living, giving those who abide by them a sense of human worth, have mostly had behind them, at however many removes, some religious conception of the human's place in the cosmos, some transcendental view of life's ultimate meaning. Their instauration has often been aided by mythological accounts of their origins in some deity's will, by ritual sanctions upon their validity.

A second, less generic, reason concerns the specific historical location of early capitalist development. Early modern European society was definitely not a secularised social world, peopled prevalently by individuals engrossed exclusively in worldly pursuits, and deaf to other-worldly concerns. On the contrary – Weber states – that society was pervaded by intense religious passions and preoccupations, of constant and momentous significance to individuals (117; 97–8). A culture so deeply imbued with Christianity harboured no diffuse, public tradition of secularism, presented no religiously neutral ground on which the capitalist spirit could grow as a set of wholly secular ideas. Exactly because that spirit constituted a scandal, a moral outrage from the traditional Christian viewpoint (58, 60; *68, 71*), it could only establish itself as the ethical statute of whole groups of men in so far as it had a *positive* religious sanction, and this could perforce be given it only by some non-traditional form of Christianity.

A complementary consideration was the following. There had been, at the beginning of the modern era, forms of social thought with a secular cast – though often decked out with pious but inconsequential references to the Christian heritage. In particular, some literary figures from the highly mundane society of Renaissance Italy had developed motifs from the rediscovered classical heritage into a world-view which was only vestigially Christian, and which strongly emphasised the significance of creature comfort, aesthetic delight, *and riches*. Some critics of Weber suggested that such figures constituted as many pre-Reformation spokesmen of the capitalist spirit; he, however, replied that the implications of those forms of thought for economic activity had nothing to do with modern capitalism. They favoured if anything the rationalisation of a distinctively 'budgetary' approach to economising, aiming to increase and judiciously administer one's family patrimony, not to accumulate capital through enterprising investment (85–6 f34; *194–5 f12*).

A final reason for seeking the religious premises of the capitalist spirit within Reformed Christianity was the fact (well established in Weber's time)[1] that modern capitalism had developed largely within predominantly Protestant territories, and largely at the hands of groups predominantly affiliated with Protestant denominations (30; *36*), and particularly with Calvinism (Puritanism, etc.) (195 f7; *220 f7*). Even assuming that in this historical connection some of the influences ran from economy to religion, rather than vice versa, it still made sense (in the light of Weber's methodological assumptions) to investigate influences running the other way, and in particular to try and determine whether Protestant religious thinking had influenced not directly modern capitalism itself, but rather the Ethos informing the activity of its early protagonists (83 f25; *191 f23*).

It is important to be clear about the nature of the relationship Weber tries to establish, and about the resultant constraints upon the nature of the relative proof. As we have seen, the spirit of capitalism – the 'dependent variable' in the relationship – is a set of ideas concerning the ethically appropriate way of conducting a business. At the other end of the relationship, the 'independent variable' is *also* a set of ideas, this time of a specifically religious rather than ethical nature – in particular, ideas concerning the issue of the individual's justification and his or her eternal salvation. Both variables being, then, sets of ideas, the relationship Weber tries to establish between them is one of *meaningful congruence*. Such a relationship cannot be established by, say, determining to what extent the empirical population of Protestant believers of this or that domination at a given time and in a given place overlapped with the empirical population of the early entrepreneurs. Establishing it requires, rather, that both sets of ideas be conceptualised in sharp, consistent terms, and that they then be tested for their intrinsic affinities at the level of meaning. If enough such affinities can be ascertained, the relationship is assumed to be an asymmetric one – from the religious to the ethical ideas, rather than vice versa.

The chief ground for such an assumption is a straightforward chronological matter: the religious ideas in question developed and became widely accepted *before* the capitalist spirit manifested itself in the patterns of activity of the early capitalist entrepreneurship. A subsidiary ground is internal to the demonstration of the affinity between the sets of ideas in question. As will be seen, it *makes sense* to derive the spirit of capitalism from certain features of Calvinist doctrine and their psychological implications. Weber does not even attempt the opposite exercise, and his reader may feel (I do, at any rate) that this attempt would *not* make the same kind of sense, even apart from the above matter of chronology.

This account of what Weber tries to do in *The Protestant Ethic* raises something of a difficulty. So far, I have emphatically separated the expression 'religious' from the expression 'ethical', attaching the former to one term in the postulated relationship – Protestantism – and the latter to the other – the spirit of capitalism (75; 89). Yet the title itself of the work we are discussing contradicts this view of its argument by speaking of 'the Protestant ethic'. How can we concile this contradiction?

As my next chapter will emphasise, the causal relationship Weber seeks to establish does not actually run *directly* from certain Protestant religious ideas to the spirit of capitalism (let alone from the former directly to capitalism itself, as some renderings of Weber's argument would have it). Between those two terms, a third one intervenes. Quite literally, Weber's title does not tell the whole story: it reduces what one may call a tryadic (three-term) to a dyadic (two-term) relationship, for the title starts with the intervening term rather than with the religious ideas 'upstream' of it.

As I see it, the *whole* story shows how a certain body of religious ideas (Calvinist doctrine, in particular) typically leads the believer to adopt a certain ethical posture (inner-worldly asceticism). This posture in turn – within certain groups, *already involved in the practice of business* – engenders a certain occupational ethic (the spirit of capitalism). (The words I *emphasised* above point to an assumption barely hinted at in the Weberian text, and which I shall elucidate at length in Chapter 8.)

But I have been getting ahead of myself, since it is only in Weber's discussion of Calvinism (as I read it) that the tryadic structure of his argument becomes later; and that discussion is to be reviewed in the next chapter. For the time being, let us rephrase the question in dyadic terms. What were the religious roots of the capitalist spirit? With what forms of Protestantism may the spirit of capitalism be said to be 'meaningfully congruent'? To what extent did the historical association between Protestantism and capitalist development rest (whatever *else* it did rest on) on an 'intrinsic affinity' between the beliefs characteristic of the former (or of *some* Protestant denominations) and the spirit animating the protagonists of the latter?

To use a metaphor, we are seeking among varieties of Reformed Christianity one or more whose basic creed makes them plausible defendants in a paternity suit, with the spirit of capitalism as the child whose ascendancy is to be determined. To guide our search we select the following among the features of the capitalist spirit discussed in the last chapter. Involvement in a worldly task is made central to the subject's whole existence. Methodical, rational control over one's activity over long stretches of time is enjoined. The increase in one's capital is taken as a self-justifying goal, and as the ultimate standard of an open-ended series of economising decisions. In the light of that standard, direct enjoyment of the fruits of previous success is strongly discouraged. All existent arrangements concerning one's activities and the activities of those under one's control are to be continually reviewed for their effectiveness, and revised as necessary. Throughout, the subject is to conduct himself as a self-activating, responsible entity, and to curb emotionality in his relations to associates and competitors.

We have already indicated our key criterion for adjudicating the contested paternity by using such (alas) vague terms as 'intrinsic affinity', 'meaningful congruence', and the like. We may test whether, in spite of its vagueness, this criterion can yield plausible results, by applying it in the first place to pre-Reformation, Catholic Christianity. To do so we draw on various, scattered references in *The Protestant Ethic* to medieval Catholicism, mostly meant by Weber to emphasise its contrast with Calvinism, or to counter some critics' contention that in the late Middle Ages some Catholic moral theologians had already articulated a religiously based outlook on economic activity closely akin to the spirit of capitalism.

Practically all features of that spirit suggest the implausibility of seeing Catholicism as its religious inspiration; but we must be selective and emphasise only the chief 'disaffinities'. In the Catholic religious vision, sacred and profane realities are not sharply separated and counterposed, but, on the contrary, widely over-lapped. The Church is on the one hand a visible institutional reality operating in the here and now, on the other a depository of the ultimate spiritual resource, God's saving redeeming grace. The distance between God and the layman is spanned by a whole range of intermediaries: angels, saints, priests, sacraments, holy practices, holy artifacts, holy places. This extensive interpenetration of the sacred and the profane discourages the faithful from treating the latter as a religiously neutral field, deprived of ritual significance, and open to his 'tinkering' and rearranging. Too many things possess, as it were, double citizenship, appear not just as deployable, instrumental objects but also as vessels of holy powers. On this account the Catholic vision cannot inspire and countenance an anti-traditionalist, rational attitude toward one's field of action.

While according to Weber the existence of sacraments in general bespeaks the persistence within Catholicism of magical thinking – the tendency to cope with higher forces on an *ad hoc* basis, securing their benevolence with distinct practices, rather than by the adoption of a coherent attitude towards them and the world – one sacrament in particular, penitence, imparts to the faithful's existence a piecemeal, 'hand-to-mouth' orientation, incompatible with the methodical approach to existence the spirit of capitalism enjoins. For the Catholic, grace lost can be regained through confession; in order to gain salvation, the believer need not impose upon his or her entire existence a continuous tension toward self-control, intolerant of lapses, and an acceptance of ultimate responsibility (132–3; *116–17*).

Furthermore, the Catholic vision, particularly as articulated in scholastic theology, projects an organic, hierarchical view of society, where the individual as such has little distinctive salience, and which lays narrow boundaries around his aspirations and his search for self-assertion. The chief units in the secular social order (as well as in the overlapping order of the Church) are clearly demarcated ranks, each vested with distinctive duties and claims – not individuals, who here are simply expected to perform their own rank's traditional tasks, and claim the respective privileges. The resulting bonds *vis-à-vis* one's associates are likely to be of a strongly concrete, personal nature, and to have a high emotional content. There is no allowance, within this social imagery, for the 'treatment of people as resources' (Tom Burns's definition of 'organising' as a distinctive form of social activity), and for the attendant reduction in the emotional content of social relations which the capitalist spirit enjoins upon the entrepreneur in the interest of an impersonal, objective pursuit of the firm's success.

On all these counts, then, the traditional Catholic vision appears very unlikely to have assisted the development of the spirit of capitalism. Weber also discounts the claim by critics that some late medieval variants of Catholic moral theology had lent such assistance. At most, the theological texts in question (many of them originating from thirteenth- and fourteenth-century Florence) afford businessmen the spiritual relief of a sophisticated *excuse* for engaging in some novel practices of a capitalistic nature. The point of such teachings is the making of allowances, the relaxing or suspending of moral rules, in order to accommodate this or that peculiar contingency of business-making (256 f236; *267–8 f42*). None of this amounts to a positive religious and moral justification for entrepreneurship, a forceful, unapologetic moral charter for the businessman's calling. Thus, these texts constitute no proof at all (Weber holds) of an intrinsic compatibility between the Catholic religious vision and something akin to the spirit of capitalism; much less do they suggest that the former, in some of its manifestations, led to the development of the latter. Indeed, their distinctly latitudinarian, permissive tone confirms that there was no place for that development in the central Catholic vision, of which they constituted a late, marginal variant (95–6 f50; *202 f29*).

However, Weber also considered a much more significant and compelling aspect of traditional Christianity which, on the face of it, does possess a meaningful affinity with some features of the spirit of capitalism. In many Western, Catholic varieties of Christian monasticism, the religious rule by which the monks lived imposed upon them a methodical and rational approach to life and to work. The Western monk was expected to exercise a strenuous control upon himself, and an active mastery upon outside reality, and to shape the latter according to a demanding, dynamic design of perfection. The resulting pattern of conduct reveals strong affinities with the spirit of capitalism; and in fact, during the history of Western monasticism, farms and other productive undertakings owned by monasteries and operated or controlled by monks were often centres of technical innovation and economic efficiency (134–5; *118–19*).

Yet, Weber argues, the affinities in question are offset by more basic contrasts, in view of which the Western monastic variants of Christianity cannot be plausibly considered as ascendants of the capitalist spirit. In the first place, monastic rules do not have the same ethical status as the injunctions making up that spirit. The former constitute 'counsels of perfection', to which only religious *virtuosi* are expected to commit themselves; they are not binding upon the Catholic layman, or for that matter the secular priest. The spirit of capitalism, on the other hand, is a standard of moral worth in principle applicable to and mandatory for Everyman. Although of course some of its injunctions only refer to the practice of entrepreneurship as such, the dutiful, steward-like attitude toward one's economic circumstances and opportunities at the core of the notion of 'calling' is applicable to other pursuits.

In the second place (but this point is closely related to the previous one), the monk inhabits a 'world apart from the world'; even his economic activity is not intended to affect and transform the public world everyone inhabits. For these two reasons, while it is possible to see in the rules of some monastic orders a distant precedent of some components of the capitalist spirit, the latter cannot be considered a child of the former (136; *121–2*).

Having thus exemplified *negatively* the criterion of inner affinity we are to follow in searching for the religious determinants of the spirit of capitalism, we must consider the *positive* results of its application to Protestantism. At this point, however, I shall simplify drastically Weber's prolonged and outstandingly sophisticated discussion, and consider its results for only *two* major Protestant denominations, Lutheranism and Calvinism. (Many of the variants of Protestantism examined by Weber, in fact, are distinctive organisational developments of Calvinism – English Puritanism, for example – or more or less heterodox doctrinal developments of it – Quakerism, for instance.) I shall treat Lutheranism, very briefly, in the balance of this chapter, and Calvinism, at greater length, in the next.

The verdict concerning Lutheranism in our paternity suit is mixed, but on balance clearly negative. On one very significant count, Luther's innovative rendering of the Christian message reveals a distinctive affinity with the spirit of capitalism, for, according to Weber, it is Luther who (particularly in his German version of the Bible) shapes the modern concept of 'calling' (*Beruf*), and places it at the ethical centre of the individual's worldly existence. The work experience is thus cleared of the religious prejudice against it implicit in the Catholic preference for *vita contemplativa*, or in the view of labour as a curse, and of acquisitive pursuits in particular as morally tainted. To all the faithful, now, no longer just the monks, the diligent performance of one's work is held forth as a dutiful response to God's will, as the testing ground of one's moral worth.

Also, the Lutheran appeal to the 'internal forum' of one's private conscience as the ultimate seat of one's awareness of God, and the confident entrusting of one's salvation to the intimately felt experience of grace, replace the Catholic's reliance on the institutional mediation of the Church and on the visible performance of ritual and penitential obeisances, and thus affirms a religious individualism akin to the ethical individualism of the spirit of capitalism.

However, according to Weber, the Lutheran vision of *Beruf* remains tied to the medieval conception of the social order as an organic whole, composed of distinctive ranks and positions, with differentiated traditional rights and duties. Lutheranism endows with greater religious significance and greater moral dignity the fulfilment of one's occupational duties, but does not require of the subject the same dynamic tension the spirit of capitalism enjoins upon the entrepreneur seeking continuously to increase his capital. Thus, the Lutheran's conscientious commitment to his worldly station does not involve him in a strenuous effort to master and rationalise reality, to innovate. According to Weber, Luther ultimately views the acceptance of one's calling as a matter of *adapting* to an existent, traditional framework of existence (71–2; 85).

Also the ethical individualism implicit in Luther's vision has considerable limitations, particularly in the version of Lutheranism embodied in the German evangelical churches (chiefly because of the political context in which they had developed after the Reformation). The Lutheran faithful is encouraged to (as it were) turn upon himself or herself, to cultivate the religious significance of his or her individuality purely within the internal space of his or her soul. The purity of one's conscience, the strength of one's faith, become the chief ground of the individual's assurance of grace – *not* the ability to impinge upon reality, as Weber puts it, *von innen heraus* ('from the core outward'). Again, there is little dynamism in this conception of individuality, and therefore little affinity with the fervent effort to *make a difference to reality* around which the spirit of capitalism centres its design of a morally worthy existence.

Finally, in Lutheranism, the sustained emphasis on human and humane emotion as the inspiring force behind one's conduct toward God and other individuals, the focus on *feeling* as the ultimate medium and standard of the moral experience, stand in contrast with the capitalist spirit's enthronement of cool, dispassionate, calculating reason as the proper source of guidance in one's entire activity.

On these counts, in spite of its religious re-evaluation of worldly tasks, and of its emphasis on individual conscience as the ultimate locus of morality, Lutheranism appears unlikely to have constituted a suitable religious inspiration for the development of the spirit of capitalism. Only a religious vision that turns worldly reality into a field of experimentation, and the individual into a 'tensed-up being', relentlessly working that field in the pursuit of a dynamic design, could plausibly be said to have offered such an inspiration.

6
The Argument, III: The Religious Determinants Identified

In dealing with Catholicism and Lutheranism, Weber does not discuss at length the respective creeds, but concerns himself almost exclusively with the religious significance they attach to everyday activity, with their existential implications. When he discusses Calvinism, however, he explicitly raises questions of dogma, and considers at some length how Calvinism conceived the Deity, its relations to the cosmos, man's place within the latter, and his eternal destiny. In this context Weber emphasises, because of their impact upon the faithful's ethical posture, two central doctrinal features of Calvinism.

In the first place, Calvinism is distinguished from other variants of Christianity by its stark emphasis on the transcendence of God (121; *103*). God's will is the sole source of the world's existence, and the increase in God's glory the world's sole justification. Yet it is as if in the act of creation itself God had disdainfully flung the world away from Himself. God does not dwell in the world, sanctify it with His presence, manifest an interest in its developments. The world is denied the sight of God and the hearing of His voice; the 'eternal silence of infinite spaces', which frightened Pascal, conceals God from the world.

Thus the whole creation, and man himself within it, is a self-enclosed reality, a distinctive ambit of finitude, corruption, and sinfulness, from within which God's will can be feared, but not clearly perceived, much less influenced and deflected. God need not communicate with the world, or involve Himself with it, in order to have His way with it. It is not given to any creature – and thus not to man – to span the gulf between himself and the creator, apprehend his will, affect it, gain His benevolence.

But the unbridgeable distance between the world (and man) and a God thus hidden, in no way entails that the former is independent of the latter. On the contrary, it conveys God's utter sovereignty over the world, His unchallengeable mastery over its destiny. As far as man himself is concerned, this finds expression in the doctrine that God has decreed from all eternity, arbitrarily and irrevocably, each individual's eternal fate – salvation or damnation in the after-life. And this decree, which (in the eye of God himself) marks each man – even during the course of his life – as ineluctably either an elect or a damned, is not revealed to him until its consummation upon death.

This is the second distinctive doctrine of Calvinism which Weber emphasises (118ff; *98ff*). Each human being, including each faithful, is assigned by God an eternal fate which he cannot ascertain prior to death, and which he is powerless to influence. Only God's inscrutable wisdom and unchallengeable arbitrium determine the individual's eternal lot, which accordingly does not constitute a punishment or reward for his temporal doings. Not even the practice of those commandments it has pleased God to reveal in the Scriptures allows the faithful to ascertain, much less to affect, the fate assigned him. He can at most fear he is damned, or hope he is an elect.

According to Weber, these two distinctive (and overlapping) features of Calvinist dogma – the doctrines of God's transcendence and of the individual's predestination – make a momentous joint impact upon the typical faithful's existential posture; they shape decisively the ethical principles to which he is likely to orient his everyday conduct. Note that what is in question here is not only, or even primarily, the explicit moral doctrines complementing the Calvinist creed, or the latter's direct, logical implications for moral conduct (297).[1] Instead, the 'ethic' grounded on the above doctrines is determined largely in terms of the following question: On the assumption that the typical faithful is pressingly concerned with his own standing as either an elect or a damned, which way of orienting and controlling his everyday existence is he likely to find *psychologically rewarding*, whether or not the explicit doctrine sanctions it as appropriate? Phrased in another way, on what typical orientation to everyday conduct do these doctrines place a 'premium', whether or not that orientation is expressly in keeping with the doctrines' explicit content and the related official moral teachings? (246 f198; *259 f4*).

In fact, the ethical consequences Weber attributes in particular to the dogma of predestination are at some variance also with its *logical* implications, or at any rate cannot be straightforwardly deduced from that dogma alone (89 f34; *197 f12*). For, on the face of it, the faithful's awareness that an inscrutable and immutable divine decree has sealed from all eternity and for all eternity his fate of damnation or salvation, might be expected to induce in him – instead of the tense, activistic orientation of conduct (to be specified below) – a fatalistic, passive resignation, whether tinged chiefly with wishful hope or grieving fear (211 f67; *232 f66*). Or, the faithful might seek to impose upon himself a kind of studied, purposeful indifference toward the issue of his eternal fate, and conduct his existence as if that destination were of no concern to himself; for why burden one's mind with anxiety over an unknown destiny one cannot alter even if one knew it?

However plausible, these *logical* implications of the predestination dogma (showing no affinity with or conduciveness to the spirit of capitalism) do not reckon with the fact that, according to Weber, it must have been a matter of constant and burning concern to the typical Calvinist faithful, whether he was elect or damned. In turn, this concern must have engendered in him an urgent *psychological need* (211 f67; *232 f66*) to gain some assurance that God's unknown decree concerning him did in fact favour him, mark him as an elect. Further, this intense need for 'proof of election' (however implausible in view of the inscrutability of God's will) generated in the faithful, instead of fatalistic resignation or a cultivated indifference toward his own fate, a profound, besetting anxiety. Finally, this anxiety pressured the faithful into a pattern of everyday existence which would at the same time express that anxiety and relieve it (128–32; *111–15*).

In many passages of *The Protestant Ethic* – and of later works – Weber characterised the pattern in question as 'inner-worldly asceticism', an expression that calls for some clarification. 'Asceticism', to begin with, goes back to a Greek noun, meaning, literally, 'exercise', originally in the sense in which we speak of physical or athletic exercise. Accordingly, within religious discourse 'asceticism' has long meant a conception whereby the faithful engages in strenuous, protracted effort on behalf of God's purpose, seeks to operate as a dutiful, active instrument of God's own will.

Such a conception obviously presupposes a view of God as a Being endowed with a purpose and a will, embodied in an ethical message at whose service the faithful places his energies. On certain understandings of such a message, asceticism may take the form of the punctilious, exacting performance of a number of detailed, specific expectations expressing God's will. But the Calvinist God makes explicit, in the Scriptures, only some of his commands; others remain veiled by the unsurmountable distance between God and the world, by the former's silence and the latter's state of corruption. Calvinism proposes only a generic understanding of God's larger purpose in creating the world and peopling it with men: to wit, the world and men exist in order that God's own glory be increased.

Thus, in Calvinist asceticism the energies of the faithful are placed at the service of a purpose that is formal (in the sense that the Scriptures offer few explicit indications as to its content) and open-ended, dynamic (in the sense that it is to be fulfilled over time, each fulfilment serving as the premise of a further one). Any specific indications (other than the scriptural ones) as to the purposes to be served by the faithful's exertions, must be derived from the nature itself of the world God has willed into existence. For in separating the world from Himself in the act of creation, God had made it into a reality with laws and requirements of its own, which can be objectively known, and whose knowledge, if acted upon, can lead to mastery over the world itself. Such mastery over the world, then, suggests itself as the generic aim and standard of asceticism within the Calvinist vision (201 f31; *224 f30*). For, as God is the entire world's master, so it is by mastering in turn his portion of the world that the faithful can operate as God's own instrument – and thus gain some psychological assurance of his own status as an elect.

A key feature of this conception of asceticism, expressed in Weber's adjective 'inner-worldly' (*innerweltlich*) is that the practice of it must take place within the public world of everyday, mundane reality, and in principle constitutes a programme for Everyman's existence. Unlike monastic asceticism, such conception does not require (or indeed allow) the ascetic to flee the hustle and bustle of mundane concerns, to distance himself from the world by establishing himself in an inaccessible, secluded place, wearing a distinctive garb, or following a body of rules applicable only to the few individuals specifically committed to them. Rather, the Calvinist 'inner-worldly' ascetic places his energies at the service of God's purpose by expending them in the pursuit of his mundane *calling*, within the proximate social environment he shares with everybody.

Thus, while Catholicism attached only to the priest's and even more specifically the monk's calling a distinctive religious valence, Calvinism shares with Lutheranism a view of each individual's calling as the centre of his moral concerns. But Calvinism differs from Lutheranism in the nature of the religious significance it attaches to the pursuit of a calling. Typically, the Lutheran faithful expressed in the dutiful performance of his calling his awareness of and his gratitude for a state of grace otherwise attained, and otherwise known to himself. For it was given to the Lutheran to keep in touch with God, as it were, and to reassure himself as to the state of his soul, through the immediacy of his innermost feelings, the intensity of his prayerful confidence in God's loving benevolence (130; *114*).

But for the Calvinist all feelings of proximity to, let alone intimacy with, God are absurd and blasphemous, and any assurance one can derive from them tainted and deceptive; above all, any confident feeling of mystical oneness with God constitutes an irresponsible denial of the individual's despicable lowliness and insignificance in God's sight. Finally, Calvinism reduces the significance of cult and ritual, of the sacraments, of ecclesiastical structures, of the priestly estate, much more drastically than Lutheranism, because of its emphasis on the gulf between God and all human experiences, including those of a religious nature.

Thus, to express it crudely, all the Calvinist faithful's ethical eggs were placed in the basket of his calling. *Only* from sustaining a correct ethical orientation to his calling could he derive some psychological assurance of his election (an assurance, let us remember, without any doctrinal warrant). He could think himself an elect to the extent that he conducted himself in his calling as an elect would.

But *how* would that be? According to Weber, the basic answer to this question was the following: the elect treats the world, in and through his calling, as much as possible as God himself does. Given that the Calvinist God is a hidden and silent one, this answer seems to provide little guidance – until one remembers that God's hiddenness and silence are an aspect of his transcendence over the world, of his aloof, detached mastery over it; and that a conception of the world as a self-standing (though not self-generating) reality, as the setting of lawful, knowable patterns and developments, complements that doctrine of God's transcendence.

Given this conception of both God and the world, then, the faithful can pattern his own relation to the world after God's own relation to it – and operate as God's active instrument – by treating the world as a reality wholly separate from God, deprived of mystery, of symbolic significances, of magical evidences of God's wisdom and of mystical lines of access to His will. Instead, he who would behave as an elect must treat the world as a set of resistant objects and contingent arrangements, and test against it his capacity for mastering and ordering reality. Thus the only posture toward the world compatible with an individual's status as an elect, and in maintaining which he can assuage his anxiety over his eternal destiny, is that of a *maître et possesseur* (200 f31; *224 f30*).

If we return for a moment to the contrast between the Lutheran and the Calvinist conception of the calling, and seek to characterise it with a metaphor, we might say that to the Lutheran his calling appeared as a *portion of space* within God's own architecture of the social order, and that he took it upon himself duly to fill that space (169; *160*). To the Calvinist, however, his calling appeared more as a *phase in time*, stretched between the moment of his own appearance on earth and that of his death, and which he treated as an open-ended task, a *chance to prove himself* (133–4; *117–18*).

Put in another way, the Lutheran surrendered himself to his calling, taken as a given, in order to express his grateful confidence in a God who spoke to him in the intimacy of his heart. The Calvinist, instead, struggled to master his calling under the pressure of his anxiety over the fate decreed for him by an inaccessible God. To him his calling was not (as it was to the Lutheran) a self-contained, definite script awaiting to be dutifully enacted; but an open challenge, in the confrontation with which his chief resource was his own ability to maintain a tension, to renew it every instance it was discharged (134; *118*). Thus the Calvinist had to put every moment of time to use through responsible, relentless activity, treating every past attainment as the premise of a future one (214 f74; *234 f73*).

This intensely dynamic relation of the Calvinist's to his calling is reinforced by other ethical implications of his creed. In particular, the doctrine of predestination tends to induce in each individual an acute sense of his apartness from others. For not only is he beset by his anxiety over his own spiritual standing; he also knows that each of his associates, including his closest relatives and familiars, may be among the damned (122–4; *106–7*). This awareness induces him to keep all associates at a certain distance, to curb spontaneity and familiarity in dealing with them; but as this tendency makes itself felt at both ends of each interpersonal relation, it progressively isolates all individuals from one another. Their mutual dealings tend to take on the same tone of aloofness as all other contacts with reality, and become subject to the same search for rational mastery (126; *109*).

Consider, furthermore, that the Calvinist faithful has available no sacramental means of relieving his sense of sin, of washing away moral guilt. This puts a further premium on his ability to plan and control his existence over long stretches of time. Optimally, the whole arc of his adult existence should be, as it were, stretched to a uniform extent, should witness a continuous, coherent design of perfection. Only in this way can his conduct afford him the psychological assurance of election he craves (132–3; *116–17*).

We can now see how many burdens the Calvinist inner-worldly asceticism imposes on the individual who seeks to conduct himself as the active instrument of God's will in and over the world. He is himself part of the world, and as such it is not given to him to feel at one with God, to submerge mystically his own existence in His; and his commitment to mastering the world on behalf of God's purpose must mean in the first place a commitment to self-mastery (135; *119*). The individual must control and repress whatever in him reflects the world's sinfulness and corruption: any tendency to engage in effort only in spurts, and then slacken; any complacent treatment of past attainments as ends in themselves; any spontaneous, unreflected attachment to familiar, comfortable, emotionally gratifying arrangements; any carefree enjoyment of the present for its own sake; any reliance for guidance in his conduct on unreflecting feeling or unexamined routine; any temptation to blame his own failings on circumstances or fate rather than his own inadequacies (138–9; *123–4*).

In the light of the doctrines of God's transcendence and of predestination, there is something absurd in the inner-worldly ascetic labouring away to be an instrument of God's purpose. For ultimately God will have his way with the world, and with each man, both through the elect's salvation and the damned's perdition, so that in a sense no individual really has any choice but to be God's instrument. In view of this, what makes distinctive the elect's inescapable involvement in and subjection to God's purpose, is exclusively a set of personal qualities displayed in the performance of his calling, and already implied in the psychological burdens listed above. The elect is active, not passive; his activity is directed by his intellect, not by habit or feeling; the timespan of his intention and his effort is lengthy, not brief; his activity is continuous, not intermittent; he takes charge of his life, does not drift nor does he trust events to go his way; he plans his existence and takes responsibility for its temporal outcome, does not bless or curse fate; he struggles to impose order and control over the things and people surrounding him, does not allow or expect them to determine him (122–3; *104–5*). Note that, on the one hand, all these qualities express the individual's innermost subjectivity, his 'moral fibre'; on the other, they all bear upon his relation to a reality outside himself, and must prove themselves in the objective impact the individual makes on that reality. Their ultimate measure is exactly the extent of that impact, the degree of its correspondence with the individual's intention.

I have already referred to the expression *von innen heraus*, from the core outward, by which Weber conveys the bi-polarity of this conception, its reference both to the individual on one side and to the surrounding reality on the other. Fundamentally, what conveys to the Calvinist faithful the sense that he is an elect can only be his ability to stand over against reality, to distance himself from it, and thus to shape it forcefully from outside (132; *116*), to make a difference to it, rather than merging with it, trying to reflect its condition within himself, adapting to it. A subjectivity centred on the cultivation of elevating thoughts and the feeling of lofty emotions, or for that matter one expressing (for instance, through charitable activity) an attitude of sympathy toward and participation with others – such conceptions are fundamentally opposed to the one Weber imputes to Calvinism, characterised by an active tension between the individual and a world of objects (comprising also other individuals).

As we have seen, although its derivation from Calvinist doctrine is complex, and indeed tortuous, at bottom this conception expresses a rather simple intuition. The elect proves himself an elect, to the extent that his conduct is God-like, in the sense of relating to the world (including the individual himself) as God himself does. Hence the characteristic emphasis on mastery, distance, and a long time perspective.

So far this chapter has dealt with the connection between some central features of Calvinist doctrine and the distinctive ethical posture they induce the typical believer to take. As I shall emphasise in the next chapter, the connection is a complex one, resulting from the joint effect of two component relationships. On the one hand, the predestination dogma, by engendering the faithful's 'need for proof of election', *cranks up the tension* in him; on the other, to this tensed-up individual the doctrine of God's transcendence *opens up the world* as a thoroughly objectified, profaned, manipulable field for purposeful action (201 f31; *224 f30*).

There is some asymmetry in the logical status of these two relationships. The second one, it seems to me, is more direct and more logical than the first: a world to which no sacred significance and valences are attached is by the same token (from a religious point of view) a manipulable world. Perhaps for this reason, while clearly postulating this relationship, *The Protestant Ethic* does not discuss it at length.

The other relationship – between the predestination doctrine and, as I have called it, the 'tensing-up' of the individual – is less direct, more contingent. Weber insists that it cannot be derived straightforwardly from the doctrine itself, which could have yielded effects very different from the 'energising' of the typical believer. As he insists, this relationship is mediated psychologically, and *The Protestant Ethic* suggests various intervening elements in it. In particular, it emphasises that in early modern Europe the question of the individual's eternal fate (still) powerfully exercised the minds of most people; and he appeals to common sense in arguing that, specifically, the typical Calvinist could not simply abandon his own fate to God's inscrutable and immutable decree, and refuse to worry about it, but *had to* grope toward some proof of his own election, however doubtful from a strictly doctrinal viewpoint. He also produces some evidence from theological statements and pastoral literature to the effect that, unable to attain assurance from ecclesiastical mediation and ritual practices, the Calvinist faithful could only assuage his need by sustaining an ascetic conduct in his worldly calling.

Composite as it is, the argument connecting Calvinist doctrine with inner-worldly asceticism only constitutes the *first half* of the thesis I am restating in this chapter. As Weber says at one point, 'after seeking in the foregoing to outline the religious foundations of the [Calvinist] conception of calling, we must now trace its impact upon business life' (164; *153*). As indicated above, the expression 'the Protestant ethic and the spirit of capitalism' phrases the *second half* of the thesis. Here, to employ again our homely metaphor, Weber pronounces judgement against inner-worldly asceticism in the suit concerning the (religious) paternity of the spirit of capitalism.

I shall deal briefly with this part of the thesis. Although Weber strengthens it by referring to some pastoral writings where inner-worldly asceticism is clearly (though not in so many words) brought to bear upon business life, he seems to me to rest his case chiefly on the numerous and significant 'meaningful correspondences' between inner-worldly asceticism on the one hand and the capitalist spirit on the other. I shall restate this case accordingly.

Weber himself summarises as follows some important meaningful correspondences, and their bearing upon his argument:

> The religious evaluation of relentless, steady, systematic work in one's worldly calling as the highest medium of asceticism, and as offering at the same time the safest and most visible proof of the purity of . . . a man's faith, must have constituted the most powerful instrument [*Hebel*] for the affirmation of the conception of life which I have named the 'spirit' of capitalism. (180; *172*)

The central connection, as I see it, concerns that disposition to make a responsible, exacting use of time, as a succession of exertions each yielding the premise of the next, which I have emphasised in my rendering of inner-worldly asceticism. For this disposition fulfils a key ethical requirement of entrepreneurship. As shown in Chapter 2, the goal of the modern capitalist enterprise is to sustain profitability over an indefinite succession of business operations, and such a goal can only be met through the entrepreneur's 'relentless, steady, systematic activity'. For here not only the acquisition of primary inputs and the disposition of output are of importance, but each moment in the intervening process, since the typical enterprise operates continuously, each moment's surplus functioning as the premise of the successful completion of the next phase in the operation. Double-entry book-keeping, which treats every moment in the process of capital accumulation and deployment as a potentially surplus-generating act of exchange, gives material expression to this attitude toward time. Such an attitude, according to Weber, was considered *ethically binding*, not just expedient, by early entrepreneurial personnel; and (originally) was so considered because inner-worldly asceticism accorded it a religious sanction, treated it as a central aspect of the elect's dutiful commitment to his calling, and thus (if sustained) as a psychologically reassuring (if theologically unwarranted) indication of his good spiritual standing.

But the typical entrepreneur must strive toward a *maximal* rate of return on his assets, not just any rate whatever. This orientation is paralleled, within the Calvinist conception of calling, by the elect's striving to order reality in a dynamic, open-ended fashion, rather than accepting any given arrangement as final. Put in another way, what is enjoined upon the Calvinist faithful by his anxious search for an assurance of salvation is *the activity itself of ordering*, rather than the acceptance of or the adaptation to any given pattern of order.

A related, significant correspondence between inner-worldly asceticism and the spirit of capitalism lies in the fact that the former discourages the individual from immediately enjoying the fruits of his own activity (lest he be corrupted by them); while the latter (as we have seen) commits every capital increment to the production of further increments, and thus forbids the entrepreneur to assign his profit to the direct satisfaction of consumption needs. The Calvinist *Berufsmensch* (i.e. man identified with his calling) is an abstemious person, who refrains from immediate gratification (176; *166*). In a business context, this attitude commands the entrepreneur to seek, first and foremost, capital accumulation through continuous investment. At the core of *both* ethical commands stands the steward-like attitude toward his own resources enjoined upon the individual: all his energies must serve the *raison d'être* of those resources, their optimal utilisation and continuous increase.

I have suggested above that inner-worldly asceticism urges the individual to cultivate certain subjective qualities not for their own sake, not because their possession marks a 'beautiful soul', but as modalities and instruments of his responsible impact upon objective reality. The view of the latter as presenting objective opportunities, while at the same time constraining action, and the consequent emphasis upon the elect's clear-eyed awareness of the situation in which he operates, find precise parallels in the spirit of capitalism. As we have seen in Chapter 4, the entrepreneur's stewardship of his own resources should not express itself as sheer retentiveness and possessiveness, nor as the rentier-like expectation that his possessions will work for him. Rather, the entrepreneur operates as such within a competitive environment, which he must continuously monitor in order to meet the challenge presented by its objective developments. Thus, while a keen, calculating control over his own resources is at the heart of entrepreneurial activity, the latter is finalised to the external, objective test of competitiveness and profitability (181–2; *172*).

To meet this test, the spirit of capitalism commands the entrepreneur to control in his dealings, and as far as possible repress, any 'all-too-human' feelings to solidarity, attachment and sympathy toward both his collaborators in the firm, and his suppliers, customers and competitors. (As the young Marx phrased it, 'if you want to be *oekonomisch*, you must spare yourself any concern with the common interest, any compassion and trust'.) In this sense – as well as in others – the entrepreneur is ethically authorised, indeed commanded, to act individualistically. Again, this command corresponds closely with an implication of the predestination dogma. As we have seen, since his associates may well be among the damned, he who would prove himself an elect should conduct himself toward them in a detached manner, restrain emotional impulses of sympathy and solidarity toward them. At the same time it would be wrong to adopt toward them a posture of hostility: the proper one is rather one of formal correctness, styling most inter-personal relations as akin to those of a contractual nature. In turn this position accords with that scrupulous observance of one's legal obligations (no more, no less) that the capitalist spirit enjoins on the entrepreneur.

A final correspondence concerns the attitudes toward change, respectively of the properly-spirited entrepreneur and of the Calvinist *Berufsmensch*. The latter, as we have seen, treats the material and social givens of his existence as lacking any specifically religious sanction, and thus considers them as purely matter-of-fact arrangements, constantly open to improvement. The resultant urge to experiment and innovate precisely matches the injunction the spirit of capitalism places upon the entrepreneur, to review and improve constantly his firm's production processes and organisation. In other terms, both roles – that of the Calvinist inner-worldly ascetic and that of the entrepreneur – have a *dynamic* ethical content, in keeping with other correspondences between them observed above; in particular, with a view of time as a medium of continuous rational operation, and a steward-like conception of one's talents and possessions (178; *170*).

As I read Weber's argument, his demonstration of the critical role played by inner-worldly asceticism in engendering the spirit of capitalism rests primarily on the above multiple and significant 'meaningful correspondences' between the two constructs. Notice, however, that Weber wants to establish a *contingent*, not a *logical* relationship between the two (lest it be objected that he proved his argument simply by defining its terms). For this reason, I believe, he presents to us the spirit of capitalism as a *secular* ethic, and uses to characterise it Benjamin Franklin's texts, which lack religious overtones; he also emphasises that, whatever its religious underpinnings, the spirit of capitalism was to become part of an ethical system as distinctively a-religious as utilitarianism.

Another indication that, for Weber, the relationship in question is a contingent one, is the fact that he connects with inner-worldly asceticism *different* ethical design for different callings. Thus, for instance, some implications of inner-worldly asceticism apply both to employers and to workers: in particular, the injunction to perform diligently one's activities and to be open to innovations. But other implications only apply to the worker; this is the case, obviously, with the injunction to comply diligently and dutifully with the directives of one's employer.

All the same, Weber's argument affirms a particularly close relationship, one of near-identity, between inner-worldly asceticism and the spirit of capitalism. As he writes, when restating the argument toward the end:

> Let the reader now reconsider Franklin's text quoted at the beginning of this essay, and he will see that the essential elements of the orientation designated there as 'spirit of capitalism' are the very ones which, in the foregoing account, make up the Puritan ethic of the calling, minus however their religious foundation, which in Franklin was already dead. (187; *180*)

The capitalist spirit, at bottom, *is* inner-worldly asceticism seen in its bearing upon entrepreneurial pursuits. Or, to phrase it with an expression of Goethe's that Weber employs frequently and significantly in *The Protestant Ethic* and elsewhere, there is between these two terms a uniquely strong 'elective affinity'.[2]

Weber, as I have already indicated, does search within pastoral Protestant literature for implicit or explicit linkages between an ascetic conception of the calling and the specific demands and opportunities of business activity. He produces texts where profits are viewed as evidence of God's benevolence toward the businessman; or where the latter is urged not to turn those profits into objects of consumption or of ostentation; or where he is urged to work tirelessly, and to specialise in a given line of work (e.g. 166–7, 170–1, 172, 179; *156, 161, 163, 171*). But in my view these textual supports should not be made to bear too much empirical weight, and should be seen largely as exemplifying an argument resting, as I suggested, on comparisons between 'ideal-type' constructs.

The Protestant Ethic's central argument, just restated in this chapter, is complemented by another in a shorter, companion essay, whose title, 'The Protestant Sects and the Spirit of Capitalism' points to its direct bearing on our topic.[3]

Weber first published 'The Protestant Sects' (in two versions) in 1906. In writing it, he made much use of the opportunity he had had in the previous year, during his trip to the United States, to become familiar both with the historical record and with the lingering reality of American Protestant sect life. In 1920 he considerably enlarged and modified that text and republished it next to *The Protestant Ethic* in his collected essays in the sociology of religion. As in the case of *The Protestant Ethic*, the following, brief comments will refer to this later version, prepared shortly before Weber's death.

It is important to see precisely in what respect and to what extent 'Sects' adds to the argument in *The Protestant Ethic*. The two essays share the view (which the latter essay had sought to establish and which the former treats as an assumption) that an ethical vision characterised as inner-worldly asceticism had supplied the religious premises of the development of the spirit of capitalism. They also share the intent of grounding in turn that ethical vision in the historical matrix of post-Reformation Christianity. However, the search led, in the two cases, to different though compatible and indeed complementary findings.

According to *The Protestant Ethic* (as we have just seen) the Calvinist predestination dogma engendered in the faithful an intense psychological need to prove himself an elect. In a world 'profaned' and objectified by the emphasis on God's transcendence, such need was both expressed and relieved by a relentless, methodical search for mastery over one's worldly circumstances through the practice of a calling.

The faithful's need for *proof of election* – Weber repeatedly writes, in both these texts – was the pivot of the whole argument (140, 141; *125, 126*). But, if so, one could wonder whether such need might be engendered *otherwise* than as a consequence of the predestination dogma. 'The Protestant Sects' gives a positive and (relatively) detailed answer to this question, by seeking an alternative determinant of that same need chiefly in the *organisational structure* of some Protestant groupings, rather than in the content of their belief systems.

Actually, the groupings discussed in 'The Protestant Sects' – chiefly a number of Baptist denominations, plus the Quakers, and a few similar sects – professed creeds largely shaped by Calvin's version of Christianity, and which in some cases even comprised the predestination dogma. But, as Weber saw it, they generated and cultivated in their faithful a need for proof of election principally as a result of their constitution, through the distinctive nature of the bonds between the groupings and their individual members, and among the latter.

Weber brings these variables into focus by characterising such groupings as sects. Sociologically, sects are defined chiefly by the fact that they view themselves as communities of individuals who have embraced Grace and jointly made a special commitment to God. Unlike churches, which are *inclusive* groupings – that is, admit (and sometimes claim) as members all individuals not somehow disqualified for membership or previously expelled from it – sects are *exclusive* groupings. That is, would-be members must possess distinctive religious qualifications, such that children are often excluded from membership, which requires adult baptism or other evidence of a conscious will to be admitted. Furthermore, the sects discussed in 'The Protestant Sects' require that a special quality and intensity of religious commitment be continuously sustained and affirmed by the members' exacting, exemplary practice of morality in all aspects of their private and public existence. To this end, they subject their members (that is, members subject to one another) to a particularly searching and demanding discipline (*Zucht*). For instance, they monitor their everyday existence and their standing in the eye of the environing secular community, prior to admitting them to each major religious ceremony, in order to preserve the latter's purity.

A sect's members must thus constitute, *as a body*, a living, active embodiment of the sect's distinctive pattern of self-sanctification. (It is, incidentally, the resulting, proud and jealous distinctiveness of the group *vis-à-vis* the larger society that one associates with the notion of 'sectarianism'.) Every member who fails to abide by the pattern threatens the whole group's assurance of its unique standing in the eye of God, violates the solidarity the 'children of the light' must sustain if they are to witness jointly the righteousness of their mode of existence, their faithfulness to God's command.

In this manner, whatever the specific intent of its doctrines, a sect engenders and maintains in its members that *active urge to prove themselves* which, as we have just seen, constitutes the dynamic core of inner-worldly asceticism. Within the Protestant sects discussed by Weber, around the time of the development of early capitalism (first in Europe, then in the United States), such 'proof' was given by members primarily through their performance in their calling: here they were expected to exhibit habits of hard work, thrift, honesty, scrupulous reliability in trade dealings. In the context of business occupations, such habits constituted the characteriological makings of success; among other reasons, because they made the individual credit-worthy, and led him systematically to re-invest his profits in the business. The historical record of such sects confirms this.

> The sect (or conventicle) member, in order to be admitted into the circle of the community, had to have determinate qualities, the possession of which was of significance for the development of modern capitalism . . . And in order to hold his own in that circle, he continually had to *prove* his possession of such qualities, which were constantly and steadily cultivated by him. Indeed . . . both his salvation in the hereafter, and his whole social existence in the here-and-now, depended on such 'proof'. According to all experience, there is no stronger instrument for

the cultivation of certain qualities than the urge to maintain one's standing in the midst of one's associates. (296)[4]

In this way, by subjecting their members to the pressures and demands of a close circle of associates in sainthood, and by rewarding them accordingly with the esteem and the solidarity of those associates, the Protestant sects, according to Weber, placed a premium on the individual's disposition to organise coherently and control conscientiously his own conduct. They thereby cultivated those very qualities that Calvinist doctrine generated in the faithful by means of their anxiety over their own eternal fate.

In particular, though the bonds of sect membership were strong, the habits such membership promoted engendered in individuals a strong sense of self-reliance and responsibility. As a grouping of religious *virtuosi* intent on proving themselves to one another, and on jointly witnessing their righteousness to outsiders, the sect alimented in members a strong feeling of individuality, an aversion from excessive mutual reliance. Each had to stand on his own feet, as an exemplar of the validity of the sect's distinctive moral design for living. Each had to display his moral worth *von innen heraus*, demonstrate his piety and saintliness in his everyday activity.

7
Some Comments on the Argument

I should like to characterise the central argument in *The Protestant Ethic*, restated in Chapters 4–6 above, as being *partial*, *complex* and *momentous*. My comments below on each of these characterisations should help the reader to grasp the significance of the argument in question, as well as to relate it correctly both to other aspects of Weber's work and to other author's accounts of matters relevant to *The Protestant Ethic*'s theme.

I call Weber's argument *partial* because it addresses a single (21; 27), distinctive and (relatively speaking) minor aspect of a very large historical problem: how to account for the genesis of modern capitalism. This is, in turn, a distinctive problem with respect to those of accounting for later phases in capitalist development, or of explaining how, once established, the capitalist system functions and maintains itself.

As to the problem of the genesis of modern capitalism, Weber insists that any reasonably adequate account would have to include a vast matrix of causes, including material premises, institutional conditions, diverse and sometimes highly contingent flows of events. As I have briefly shown in Chapter 3, he occasionally reviews this causal matrix, but is always careful to point out that any such review is perforce selective, never truly comprehensive.

Within a large complex of causes, then, *The Protestant Ethic* singles out for attention one set of causal processes, those eventuating in the formation of a relatively large body of entrepreneurs, who undertook to exploit the opportunities for commercial and productive innovation and for capital accumulation opening up in seventeenth-century Europe. Within this set, Weber *further* selects one aspect, the emergence of an historically unprecedented, indeed on the face of it 'scandalous', ethical construction of the modes of conduct that the single-minded, rational pursuit of profit imposes upon the economising agent.

Finally, having designated as spirit of capitalism this *explanandum*, Weber undertakes to investigate only its religious sources. In fact, not all of these. He suggests that also the Western conception of the monk's calling may have favoured the formation of the capitalist spirit (87 f34; *196 f12*); but prefers to emphasise the difference between that conception and inner-worldly asceticism, and the latter's unique causal significance. As we have seen, he finally identifies two distinct though compatible (and overlapping) processes through which Reformed Christianity assisted in the formation of the spirit of capitalism: the implications of Calvinist doctrine for the faithful's ethical posture; and the formation of sects generating in their members a need to prove themselves morally worthy in their everyday conduct.

Thus, Weber's central argument addresses a problem arrived at after a number of conscious thematic selections (140; *125*). In *this* sense the argument is partial – indeed, highly so. For while Weber argues that the above causal relation is a direct and significant one, clearly its bearing on the larger problems (the formation of early entrepreneurship or, even more, the genesis of modern capitalism) is mediated, and above all limited. One may sum up the matter by saying that Calvinism was a necessary though not sufficient condition for the rise of modern capitalism. But this formula, while correct, makes the relationship appear more direct than it seemed to Weber himself; and above all it hides the quantitative disproportion between the *explanans* and the *explanandum*. I mean by this, once more, that any reasonable account of the latter would have to involve many more additional conditions.

Besides being *thematically* partial, the argument in *The Protestant Ethic* is also *methodologically* so. As I have insisted, while occasionally making recourse to other research approaches, ultimately Weber rests his argument on the claim that there exist many significant 'meaningful correspondences' between ideal-typical constructs, sets of coherently formulated ideas. As I read it, his key argument concerns three such sets: the Calvinist conception of God and of God's relation to creatures; the Protestant ethic of inner-worldly asceticism; and the spirit of capitalism.

Weber makes no sustained attempt to back up the argument by

means of alternative research strategies. He does not, for instance, investigate systematically the correlation between the territorial spread of Calvinism and the geographical distribution of early capitalist enterprises. He uses pastoral writings from Reformed churches to point to some of the above meaningful correspondences, and particularly some presumptive psychological connections between the holding of certain doctrinal views and the adherence to an ethical programme for systematising one's life conduct. But he does not seek to establish how wide was the readership of such writings among clergy and laity, much less to determine whether and to what extent they reflected concretely felt preoccupations of the faithful and how these in turn affected their conduct. Nor does *The Protestant Ethic* seek to document, say through biographies and personal documents, whether an urgent anxiety over their fate in the after-life actually 'drove into entrepreneurship' particularly devout and sensitive Calvinists.[1]

Naturally these methodological alternatives (of some of which Weber was aware: cf. 245–6 f197; *259 f3*) were extremely difficult to pursue, and it is very doubtful whether pursuing them would have conclusively settled the matter one way or another; and this, I think, justifies Weber's deciding not to pursue them. Yet it is important to be aware of such alternatives, for the very richness of the historical material on which *The Protestant Ethic* draws obscures somewhat the narrowness of its methodological ground. I have mentioned one potentially serious consequence of it: the ascertainment of 'meaningful correspondences' between sets of ideas said to stand in a causal relation to one another – such as the ethic of inner-worldly asceticism and the spirit of capitalism – may awaken the suspicion that the relationship is in fact a non-contingent one, one set of ideas being a subset of the other, or formed by logical extensions of its components.

Besides being partial, in the senses indicated, Weber's argument is highly *complex*. I mean by this that on any reasonable account it comprises a number of discrete points, connected by a correspondingly high number of steps or transitions.

Again, my insistence above on separating conceptually Calvinist doctrine from Protestant ethic, and connecting them with one another before connecting both with the spirit of capitalism, points to such complexity. Previous chapters have given further indications of its extent. For instance, in order to counter the view that the

Reformation favoured capitalism by suspending (rather than modifying and strengthening) ethical preoccupations concerning business activity, Weber has to postulate that in early modern Europe individuals were (still) deeply and sincerely concerned with the nature of the after-life and their own destination within it (117; *97*). At various points, in order to establish connections between one step and another in his reasoning, Weber must introduce psychological assumptions into it (e.g. 211 f67; *232 f66*).

My own account has further increased the argument's complexity by suggesting that not just the predestination dogma, but a view of the world as a wholly profane reality, are required to make credible the rationalising and energising impact of Calvinist doctrine upon economic activity. I have also emphasised other components of Weber's thinking more than he does himself – in particular, the conception of time as a continuous medium for action, to be made use of in all its moments, which in my view constitutes one of the most significant commonalities between inner-worldly asceticism and the spirit of capitalism.

Finally, as we have seen, in 'The Protestant Sects and the Spirit of Capitalism' Weber juxtaposes to an argument focused on *religious ideas* (previously developed in *The Protestant Ethic*) one focused on *patterns of religious association*. The latter, too, embody religious ideas; but the new argument stresses not so much the resultant psychological pressures upon individuals, as their constant social validation by means of positive and negative sanctions, in particular those based on a sect's fundamental property of selectively accepting or excluding individuals as members.

This last example highlights one methodological implication of the argument's complexity. Only because in *The Protestant Ethic* the 'need to prove oneself' is treated as a conceptually distinctive component, could Weber – in the later essay – ask himself whether such a need could be generated *otherwise* than through the Calvinist's anxiety over his eternal fate, and answer that it could be generated by a religious group's constitutional structure and the resultant forms of discipline (*Zucht*). That need, then, becomes the 'equifinal' product of two different (though compatible) flows of causal influences.

In this sense, the argument's complexity strengthens it, because it makes a given step less dependent on a given sequence of antecedents (in so far as more than one sequence leads to the same step).

However, there is a sense in which complexity, while enriching the argument, may weaken it. As the number of conceptually discrete components grows, the argument's structure becomes more fragile, particularly in so far as some of the several points may be challenged as to the weight of the evidence (if any) behind them. To refer back to previous indications of its complexity, the argument is weakened by the fact that at various points it introduces unsubstantiated (though generally very credible) psychological assumptions, or by the fact that (for instance) Weber simply *asserts* that concerns over the after-life occupied a central position within the mentality of early modern European populations.

I call Weber's argument *momentous* in order to suggest that, paradoxically, its partiality (in the sense specified above) increased its significance, its theoretical leverage. As we have seen, the argument does not aim to establish a set of conditions *sufficient* to account for the rise of early capitalist entrepreneurship, let alone the larger phenomenon of the genesis of modern capitalism. But surely the point of the argument is, rather, that the causal relationship it claimed to have established had a *necessary* part to play in those phenomena.

How powerful this claim is can be shown by formulating it curtly and sharply: no capitalist development without an entrepreneurial class; no entrepreneurial class without a moral charter; no moral charter without religious premises. In other words, a specifically *religious* development (Calvin's new Christian vision) is claimed to have made an indispensable, positive difference to a development taking place in the *economic* sphere, and from which were to flow numerous, diverse, dramatic consequences for the European (and then the world) social order at large, in all its aspects (including religious ones . . .).

This conclusion is already significant as a contribution to the explanation of a course of events of the greatest historical import. It becomes *momentous* (in the sense intended here) in view of its wider theoretical implications, which of course Weber envisaged from the beginning. These implications are best seen in the context of a contrast, (often rehearsed by sociologists, and not to be reviewed here)[2] between Weber's thought and Karl Marx's. What I called the partiality of Weber's argument implies that his and Marx's accounts of the genesis of modern capitalism differ only marginally. Yet that marginal difference impinges significantly on wider theoretical issues concerning, say, the 'role of ideas' in socio-historical causation, the bases of group identity, or the appropriate ways to conceptualise different kinds of social interests and their relations.

As far as these questions are concerned, Weber himself thought that *The Protestant Ethic* decisively invalidated – through the sustained examination of a significant contrary instance – some claims advanced in his own time (and occasionally in ours) on behalf of so-called historical materialism. It undermined in particular the partitioning of the component elements of social reality into two realms – the (economic) basis and the (ideological) superstructure – and the attendant claim that the configuration of the former, resulting from the social ordering of the historically available production forces, conditions decisively – though perhaps only 'in the last instance' – the configuration of the latter (which comprises religious ideas), and that this relationship between the two realms is in principle irreversible.

Note that, according to Weber himself, this formulation, while it had behind it the authority of a famous Marxian text (the so-called 'Preface of 1859')[3] did not reflect the sophistication of Marx's own thought (237 f169; *252 f168*), and did not do justice to the potential usefulness of historical materialism as a broad research hypothesis (190; *183*). Indeed, in other writings, Weber himself explored the bearing of that hypothesis also on the relationship between economic group interests and patterns of religious thought and practice (269 f77; *277 f84*). However, he saw his own argument in *The Protestant Ethic* as invalidating historical materialism when understood as an utterly general and conclusive formulation of the structure and the laws of development of socio-historical reality (46; *56*).

We can appreciate better the momentousness of these implications of the argument if we reflect on the few indications Weber gave as to how he would address the question, 'What, *then*, brought about Calvin's version of Christianity?' (193 f5; *220 f7*). For the indications are that while Weber's answer would attribute much significance to a wide range of antecedent social conditions (including economic ones) and of doctrinal sources of Calvin's views, he definitely would also assign causal significance to an irreducible moment of sheer prophetic vision, to the imaginative resolution of a heroic confrontation with problems of ultimate meaning (120; *101*). Quite generally, religious innovation – whatever else conditions and circumscribes it, whatever else favours or contrasts its diffusion, its embodiment into articulate doctrine, institutional structure, ritual practice – always involves a creative individual's intuition and articulation of an absolute, transcendental truth on which to ground his or her search for salvation (73; *87*).

Thus Weber roots the specificity of the religious experience, at any rate at those critical junctions where new visions informing it are apprehended and originally communicated, in a fundamental and universal human predicament: the search for ultimate meaning in an ultimately meaningless world. He also claims that the (inescapably arbitrary and indeed irrational) resolution of this dilemma, when it is distinctively novel and forceful, and when diverse historical circumstances aid its transformation into a collective vision, may in turn significantly affect the course of historical events, eventuating in innovations also of a non-religious nature (or, for that matter, adding its own resistance to that of other forces resisting innovation).

Thus, the argument in *The Protestant Ethic* is not only *negatively* significant in that (according to Weber) it invalidated some key tenets of historical materialism; *positively* it establishes that, as a distinctive element in a wider matrix of causes, religious ideas may exercise leverage on many, disparate aspects and phases of the historical process (76; *90*). Here, I shall offer a brief elucidation of this point, relating back to aspects of Weber's thought already suggested in Chapter 3. (Weber's own full-scale elaboration of the same points is the main concern not just of *The Protestant Ethic*, but also of his other essays in the sociology of religion.)

The historical efficacy of religious (and other) ideas is largely contingent upon the outcome of conflict. For in order to impart their own bias to this or that aspect of the institutional structure of society, new ideas must dislodge the contrasting and resistant implications of previous ideas and of other social constraints already *in place*. Whether the resultant conflict will have a resolution favourable or unfavourable to the new ideas, however, does not depend primarily (much less exclusively) on their intrinsic content (or for that matter on that of the 'resistant' old ideas). Even the group that embraces a new set of ideas and on their behalf and in their light puts pressure on other groups, may have already possessed a collective identity based on other commonalities, little to do with religious or other ideal concerns. Although the religious ideas the group comes to share may considerably energise it and reorient its action significantly, in the ensuing mutual adjustments, negotiations and open and possibly violent confrontations between that group and others, the content itself of the ideas may play a less decisive role than *other* shared resources and commonalities of each group, the capacity of its leadership, or sheer intractable historical contingency.

For all that, in Weber's view, *ideas matter in history* (211 f67; *232 f66*) – and not just because (whatever their content) they provide symbols of affiliation and standards of membership. Their content itself does matter (21; *27*), or Weber would not have bothered to concern himself with the specific intellectual, doctrinal features of the religions he discusses, in *The Protestant Ethic* and elsewhere. For, ultimately, individuals must rely on ideas (mostly, of course, ideas proffered to or imposed on them by others) in making sense of their existence, in construing the stakes circumstances hold out to struggling groups, the sanctions they inflict on the weak and the vanquished. Religious and moral ideas, in particular, may define very differently to individuals the occasions for hope and despair, the grounds for guilt, pride or assurance, the extent to which individual and collective existence is open to the judgement and the intervention of transcendental forces, the amenability of these to passion and compassion, to reason and unreason in their relation to men.

Of course such constructions placed on reality must interact with more objective givens in ordering action, in grounding and dissolving commonalities, in fashioning and refashioning the life situations themselves of individuals. This is one reason why, while the content of ideas matters, their historical consequences, having to be mediated by the above interactions and by the mutual impact of groups oriented to different ideas, cannot be derived straightforwardly from a surface rendering of that content. Another reason is that the actors themselves must integrate that content (as *they* read it) into a wider context of tendencies, resources, and interpretive devices.

The resulting deviousness of the impact of ideas upon action (82 f23; *192 f24*) points in turn to a major aspect of Weber's wider view of the historical process: his emphasis on the unpredictability, irony, paradoxicality of cause-and-effect relationships. For, as over time the effects of certain causes go on to produce further effects, and so forth, the relation between the earlier causes and the later effects in the sequence often becomes highly opaque and twisted. Above all, the bearing of the original *intentions* upon the later *outcomes* often becomes positively bizarre and perverse (76; *90*). In the thought of Weber, this opacity of cause-and-effect relations, this perversity of intention-and-outcome relations is constitutive of the notion itself of history (and not just, as in Marx's view, of the 'pre-history' that precedes the advent of socialism), and imparts to history its distinctive tension and irony. *The Protestant Ethic* displays a whole range of aspects of this conception, which conveys an insight into the very structure of the human being, the 'excentricity'[4] of its position in the world. Consider the following aspects:

(1) *The sense of incongruity.* *The Protestant Ethic* affirms that things apparently as different as chalk and cheese (an obscure theological doctrine at one end, the institutional and material apparatus of capitalism at the other) can stand in a however remote and 'partial' relation of cause-and-effect to one another.

(2) *The autonomisation of effects.* A religious inspiration is asserted to have been indispensable to the formation of the spirit of capitalism; but then the latter, as an ethical view of the entre-preneur's calling, becomes independent of that inspiration (see Franklin's case). Also, after making an indispensable contribution to the genesis and affirmation of modern capitalism (*The Protestant Ethic* asserts), the spirit of capitalism itself becomes dispensable for the continuing operation of capitalism as a system (45; *55*).

(3) *The changing significance of persistent phenomena.* To this aspect Weber gave its sharpest expression in a lapidary sentence: 'The Puritan *wanted* to be a *Berufsmensch*. We *have no choice* but to be.' (188; *181*). A generation's moral project, embraced with a sense of its intrinsic validity (and perhaps of its religious significance) may become to later generations purely a set of tactical, expediential directives on how to adapt to objective constraints, followed purely because it would be impractical or foolish not to do so. In the context of the typology of work motivations proposed in *Economy and Society* this involves a shift from one motivational pattern to a very different one (W60; *110*).

(4) *The moral ambiguity of ideas.* All knowledge – and emphatically all evaluation – is inescapably perspectival: that is, it expresses the knowing and evaluating subject's rootedness in a specific social

and intellectual context, leading to different perceptions and interpretations of the same phenomena. For instance, to some businessmen the capitalistic rationalisation of their traditional business conduct may have been, again, a moral project, a test of their own moral stature; while upon others that same transformation may have been imposed by the competition of the former as the sole alternative to 'going under' (57; *68*). More widely, the spirit of capitalism attaches positive ethical significance to a relentless search for gain and an abstemious attitude toward the fruits of one's economic success, which previously had been universally regarded as distinctly irrational and immoral.

(5) *The tragedy of self-destruction.* Often a given original cause not only produces effects which become 'autonomous' of itself, it may also be undermined or threatened by some of those effects. Some of the Protestant divines discussed by Weber had already uneasily perceived this paradox. The godliness of their faithfuls, they wrote, assists them in gaining economic success; but then a number of them succumb to the temptation of riches, and become more and more indifferent to religion (182–3; *175*). On a grander scale, the central irony envisaged in *The Protestant Ethic* is that Calvin's vision, one manifestation of that great season of the Western religious spirit constituted by the Reformation, assisted the genesis of the capitalist spirit, and thus the development of an economic system whose hold upon the West – and later upon the whole world – contributed decisively to the advance of secularisation and thus to the withering away of Christianity. Weber sharply summarises this and similar ironies by inverting the way Goethe's Mephistopheles defines himself to Faust: 'I am the spirit that always intends the *good* and always brings about *evil*' (180; *172*). (Or, to phrase it in another way: if God is dead, He's dead by His own hand.)

The argument in *The Protestant Ethic*, then, illustrates cogently some quite general aspects of historical experience. However, Weber equally emphasises the utterly unique, epoch-making significance of the developments he reconstructs in *The Protestant Ethic*. For the advent of modern capitalism not only revolutionises the Western economy, it also works powerful effects upon all other Western social structures (which often condition and affect it in turn). Furthermore, from early on, capitalism operated as the chief determinant and beneficiary of the West's powerful expansionary thrust, which in one part of the world after another dislocated the local social and cultural structures until it reorganised the whole world into a comprehensive system, centred (for many centuries) on the West's own supremacy.

This second theme stands in the foreground of the *Vorbemerkung* Weber preposed in 1920 to the book edition of *The Protestant Ethic* and other essays in the sociology of religion (9ff; *13ff*). Here, in fact, capitalism is considered together with *other* phenomena which jointly establish the utter peculiarity of the Western historical experience.

From the West, Weber suggests, have originated a number of distinctive social and cultural phenomena, which then extended their powerful impact upon other parts of the world. In other words, what is *particular* about the West is that it formed and promoted a number of social and cultural innovations of *universal* significance. Thus, Western science displaces and replaces a variety of both vernacular and sophisticated bodies of empirical lore. The modern state becomes the pattern after which rulers all over the world seek to organise their activities. Capitalism, as we have seen, disrupts and supplants alternative material and institutional arrangements for producing and distributing material goods. Western technology at first complements, then progressively replaces, traditional, craft-based devices for performing all manner of tasks, from production to transport to warfare.

But why, Weber wonders in the *Vorbemerkung*, has it been given to the West to affect so deeply and pervasively so many institutional realms (as well as others, such as law, music, or architecture) in so many parts of the globe, some of which in each of those realms had previously developed distinctive, sophisticated, long-lasting arrangements of their own?

At first, the emphasis with which Weber attaches the label 'rational' to each of the Western achievements he reviews (*20–2; 26–8*) seems to provide an answer. 'Rationality' entails that in a given sphere of existence the institutionally prescribed modes of thought and conduct favour the conscious selection of the objectively most appropriate means to given ends, over and against the dutiful observance of traditional patterns or the spontaneous acting-out of unreflected emotions. Thus understood, rationality has the advantage of allowing actors both to plan their own course of action and to foresee others'; this in turn allows their action to impinge more predictably and efficiently on its own context.

Rational patterns of thought and conduct, furthermore, have a quality of matter-of-factness and abstractness which allows them to superimpose themselves upon locally rooted, culture-bound traditions and patterns of feeling, suppressing or restraining their significance for action. This, together with the objective effectiveness of rational patterns of action, accounts for their transferability from one larger context to another, and thus for their universality. In sum, the West's peculiar commitment to the *rationalisation* of existence accounts (on the face of it) for its success in shaping the world at large to its own image and imposing upon it its superiority.

But this is only a provisional answer, and to some extent a deceptive one. In the first place, however useful in characterising the peculiar ways of the West and accounting for their impact on other cultures and civilisations, the notion of rationalisation does not go a long way toward *explaining* those ways themselves. Also, the very notions of rationality, rationalisation, are far from univocal in their meaning (64–5; *76–7*). One can 'rationalise' a given aspect of existence, Weber says, in the light of very different criteria; and the most general of these are bound not to be themselves rational, but flow from a pre-rational (though perhaps subsequently rationalised) intuition of the ultimate ground of reality, and/or from the arbitrary attachment of primary meaning to one aspect of existence over and against others (84 f31; *194 f9*).

Finally, it would be foolish (in the light of this understanding of the term itself) to consider 'rationalisation' a uniquely Western destiny and prerogative. All major cultures and civilisations have, in their own fashion, rationalised various aspects of existence. Each of these rationalising enterprises have necessarily received their concrete significance from being carried out to this or to that extent, in this or that sphere of existence, in this or that manner. For Weber, these variant historical manifestations of the generic phenomenon of rationalisation – variants to be captured as far as possible by means of ideal-typical constructs – constitute the proper, proximate objects of investigation, both as things to be explained and in their bearing upon the explanation of other phenomena. Only such investigations can provide the beginnings of a determinate, non-generic answer to the problem posed in the *Vorbemerkung*.

The Protestant Ethic and the other essays in the sociology of religion make a twofold contribution to such an answer. On the one hand, they locate in Judaic prophecy and in the Calvinist version of Christianity the chief religious components of the (obviously very complex) matrix of causation *explaining* the particular Western mode of rationality. On the other hand, they *characterise* that mode, with special reference to its impact upon everyman's conduct of everyday existence. Here the emphasis lies on the dynamic, self-transcending nature of Western rationality, and on its tendency to *disenchant* the world, to treat it as a set of objective arrangements, to be continuously and ruthlessly tinkered with.

As can be seen, *The Protestant Ethic* develops extensively one aspect of the first contribution (the emphasis on Calvinism), and both aspects of the second contribution to what may be called 'the *Vorbemerkung* problem', and its vital bearing has frequently been commented on, often in the context of a review of Weber's other essays in the sociology of religion.[5]

There is, however, an alternative approach to determining the wider significance of *The Protestant Ethic*, rather less widely adopted in the secondary literature. My last chapter attempts to redress the balance by developing this relatively neglected approach.

8
An Alternative Historical Context

In the last chapter I have emphasised the relatively narrow methodological ground on which *The Protestant Ethic* conducts its argument. It does not reconstruct the activities of concrete historical groups, or chart the correlations between the spread of religious and moral ideas issuing from the Reformation and the diffusion of new, modern-capitalistic forms of business. It does not depict the selection processes through which entrepreneurial groups activated by the spirit of capitalism emerged and set about conducting business in a new fashion. Rather, as I have insisted, the argument rests chiefly on the identification and elucidation of meaningful correspondences between sets of ideas.

However, both *The Protestant Ethic* and other writings of Weber's contain insights into the concrete historical processes through which Calvinist doctrine generated the moral habitus of inner-worldly asceticism, and the latter became transformed into the spirit of capitalism. Above all, they discuss the nature and the vicissitudes of some social groups which served as 'carriers' of those developments.

In this final chapter I shall capitalise upon the latter discussions. Thus, once more, instead of providing an independent historical account, I shall develop a narrative framework derived from Weber's own writings, and among these chiefly from 'The City', a lengthy essay which Weber had originally intended as complementary to his comparative essays in the sociology of religion,[1] but which his editors have turned into a chapter of the posthumous part of *Economy and Society* (W 727–824; *1212–374*).

For our present purposes, the chief merit of 'The City' is that it outlines the social history of the Western bourgeoisie. For, in my view, *The Protestant Ethic* contains a 'story' which can in turn be treated as one chapter (and an extremely important chapter) within that social history. My key contention is that *The Protestant Ethic* concerns not so much the formation of a wholly new collective actor, as rather the (however radical) transformation of a pre-existent one – an urban status group already involved in the conduct of business, and on this account already possessing a distinctive (and privileged) social location within the early modern Western city.[2]

Thus, the concrete historical processes through which Calvin's vision (and the Protestant sects) contributed to the genesis of modern capitalism, are best seen against the background of an already highly differentiated and sophisticated urban social structure. It is only within this context, I contend, that *The Protestant Ethic*'s argument becomes a plausible (though implicit) account of *wie es eigentlich gewesen*, the way things actually occurred.

On this reading, in the narrative imagery underlying Weber's argument Calvinism does not operate, as it were, socially at random, turning into capitalist entrepreneurs – through the mediations we have repeatedly reviewed – individuals previously active in whatever walk of life. It has that effect only, or at any rate most prevalently, upon individuals already engaged in business, and who as such enjoy a consciousness of kind, a common legal status, and distinctive cultural orientations – not to mention distinctive economic resources and interests. As we shall see, all these commonalities are profoundly altered in so far as such individuals (under the impulse *also* of their new religious vision and the associated moral concerns) undertake to do business in a new way. Nevertheless, these alterations *presuppose* those commonalities.

If *The Protestant Ethic* and, for that matter, other writings of Weber's offer only little textual support for this reconstruction of such an 'implicit narrative', this is, I submit, because Weber took it utterly for granted that the processes he postulated had the early modern Western city as their locale, and that within the social structure of the latter the protagonists of those processes already occupied a distinctive location (249 f211; *262 f17*).[3] If, for example, we review the 'factors' Weber often lists as necessary preconditions of the rise of modern capitalism, we realise that, in early modern Europe, factors as significant as certain rational structures of law, politics and administration, a relatively sophisticated money system, and an accumulation of reliable technical information and scientific knowledge, all had their location chiefly in the urban social structure, and were mainly operated by sections of that structure's middle and upper-middle strata.

A further reason for considering *The Protestant Ethic* as a critical episode in the history of the Western bourgeoisie is that many aspects and phases of Weber's work witness to the keen interest he had in the theme of this chapter: what persists and what changes within the millennial history of the Western bourgeoisie. (In a moment I shall modify the latter term.) Let us also remember that this 'historical individual', besides being one of those unique Western social formations in which Weber had so much interest, was also the larger collective-historical entity of which he personally felt part, as I have already suggested in Chapter 1. In his inaugural lecture at Freiburg (1895) Max Weber resoundingly proclaimed: 'I am a member of the bourgeois class, I consider myself one, and I have been raised according to its views and ideals.'[4] It is true that, as the context indicates, Weber's affiliation with the *German* bourgeoisie of his time was a troubled and at times embittered one. Yet the standard itself by which he criticised his class associates was a view of the bourgeoisie more responsive to its distinctive interests and values, more committed to its peculiar historical mission.

The arrangement of the argument that follows is suggested by a sentence from the 1920 *Vorbemerkung*, worth quoting, among other reasons because a serious mistranslation in the standard English version obscures a point central to my own argument here. In this passage Weber formulates as a central theme of *The Protestant Ethic* and of his other essays in the sociology of religion 'the emergence of the Western *Buergertum* and its specific nature, which is indeed closely connected, but not simply identical, with the emergence of the capitalist organisation of labor. For there had existed *Buerger*, understood as an estate, previous to the development of Western capitalism' (18; *24*). And in a previous sentence, he remarks that 'nowhere but in the West has there been a concept of the *Buerger*, and nowhere but in the modern West that of the *bourgeoisie*' (17; *23*).

This chapter articulates, in his own terminology, Weber's summary contention that the development of the bourgeoisie proper constitutes a later, modern phase within the historical experience of a more lasting collective entity, the *Buergertum*. Its chief argument is closely based on the above sentences, and can be summarised as follows. The Western *Buergertum* is a unique historical entity which has possessed, in sequence, two vastly different collective identities: first that of an estate (let us then speak of the 'burgher estate' or 'estates'), then that of a class (let us call *only* this the 'bourgeoisie'). The transition from the former to the latter is associated with the advent of modern capitalism (and with other developments of the 'modern era', as understood in German usage, that is beginning approximately in the late sixteenth century). I shall view the argument in *The Protestant Ethic* as dealing with one specific aspect of that transition, and thus with the transformation of the Western *Buergertum* from an estate into a class.

I shall describe three major phases within the 'story' in question, the first of which sees the rise of the early burgher estate, its initial affirmation as a distinctive and significant social entity. This development occurs in a period (late tenth to eleventh century A.D.) when in Europe as a whole the characteristic politico-military and economic arrangements of feudalism are predominant, and slowly initiates an urban revival in a context where for centuries almost all significant political and social relations and cultural endeavours had been land-based, and sustained by an overwhelmingly rural economy.

Weber has little to say about some problems concerning this phase – for instance, the question of the social origins of the first inhabitants of the new medieval towns. He is much more concerned to emphasise, within the comparative framework he adopts in 'The City', that those inhabitants, whatever their social origins, established with one another very distinctive social bonds, and collectively claimed, within the larger social order, a historically unique position.

The early historical record of a number of European cities documents a phenomenon that to Weber best symbolises the novel institutional nature of the nascent (or, sometimes, *re*nascent) medieval towns. This phenomenon is the *conjuratio*: a collective oath by which a plurality of individuals *constitute* a town, and commit themselves to its defence and to the pursuit of their shared interests as its inhabitants. This is a significant development in a number of ways.

In the first place, the oath in question is a religious act, solemnised by Christian ritual. Now, Christianity is a religion that addresses individuals as such, not as members of kinship or ethnic groups. This allows it to sanction and intensify commonalities (such as those established by the *conjuratio*) which are not primordial but voluntary, are grounded on shared interests envisaged through rational argument, and are thus in an emphatic sense historical, open to redefinition. (By contrast, in the classical Indian town, highly exclusive ritual groupings continually interfere with the commonalities based on the shared locality; and in the classical Chinese town, the abiding solidarity of the lineage connects the inhabitants back to different village bases, and again prevents them from seeing themselves and one another primarily as townspeople.)

In the second place, the *conjuratio* generally constitutes the dramatic culmination of a sequence of acts of collective conspiracy and rebellion of the early medieval townsmen *vis-à-vis* the powers of the feudal lords and sometimes of their overlords, the territorial rulers. It expresses and dramatises a challenge to the existent state of things, by constituting the town as a distinctive social space whose inhabitants intend to order their own existence instead of letting others order it for them. Note, however, that the challenge is a limited, defensive one; in principle it aims not to destroy the wider framework of rule, but simply to secure the town's arranging of its own internal affairs against interference from that framework. In other words, the 'oath-takers' seek for the town not so much 'sovereignty' as 'autonomy'. (In this the medieval town typically differs from the classical *polis*; it also differs, consequently, in the lower priority it assigns to military and political pursuits, as well as in the nature of its economic base.)

Finally, the *conjuratio* is a collective act in a distinctive, emphatic sense. It conveys the intuition that singly powerless individuals can acquire power through solidarity; the franchises and immunities it seeks from outside powers are vested in the town as a corporate entity, and individuals can avail themselves of them only in their capacity as townsmen. (Again, the primordial and ritual solidarities fragmenting the ancient Chinese and Indian towns prevented them from acquiring this distinctive corporate existence.)

Whatever insights one may gain from considering closely the nature of the medieval *conjuratio*, the phenomenon itself becomes possible and gains its institutional significance only on the basis of protracted material processes, concerning primarily the physical construction of an urban settlement and the development within it of a relatively advanced division of labour, centred on economic activities distinct from and complementary to those taking place in the countryside. This allows the accumulation within the settlement of economic resources (largely in the form of specie or manufacts), part of which is mobilised for political purposes (particularly in aiding the territorial rulers to curb the power of the feudal element) and for military purposes (arming the town militia, surrounding the town with defensible walls). It is the success of these economic and politico-military processes (whether or not symbolised by a *conjuratio*) that allows the typical medieval town to assert its autonomy within a wider framework of rule, and to elaborate a highly distinctive urban structure and culture.

A second phase within our story, then, embraces those centuries (roughly, from the twelfth to the late fifteenth) during which the Western *Buergertum* attains its first major configuration as an estate, involved in the development of the increasingly significant town economy, in the making of new legal and political arrangements for the conduct of the town's internal affairs, and in the establishment of an uneasy but relatively lasting political equilibrium in the town's relations to other privileged groups.

In Weber's typology of domination, the latter achievement coincides with a distinctive variant of traditional domination, the *Staendestaat*. This is, once more, a uniquely Western phenomenon (*12; 16*): two sets of corporate holders of legitimate prerogatives of rule, the feudal estates on the one hand, the towns on the other (together with other corporate bodies, ecclesiastical and secular), formally co-operate with a central ruler and his patrimonial apparatus in the governance of relatively large territories. At the local level they exercise autonomous political prerogatives, which allow the feudatories to control and to exploit the peasantry, and the towns to promote and regulate their own economic activities and the resultant traffics. Within the larger territories, both feudatories and towns participate in the central ruler's governance by advising him on his policies and by contributing resources to their execution.

This participation takes place mostly through region- and territory-wide *Staende*: bodies formally constituted for the purpose of voicing the corporate claims of the feudal and (separately) of the town element, and of setting the terms under which both are willing to support the ruler's undertakings. To obtain that support, the ruler is constrained to acknowledge the immunities and prerogatives vested in such bodies and in their constituent social groups – including the prerogative of legitimate resistance against the ruler himself, should he unduly encroach upon the groups' privileges.

The political equilibrium maintained through these arrangements is perforce an unstable one, among other reasons because their triangular structure invites each major component (the feudal element, the town element, the ruler) to join forces with another in order to curb the pretensions of the third. Within the complex game of alliances and counteralliances that results, one may discern a broad trend: at a number of critical junctures, the towns decisively support the territorial ruler against the feudal element. Thanks to the financial, military, and intellectual assistance of the town element, many rulers, during the later decades of the *Staendestaat*, are able to prepare its supersession by a more centralised and bureaucratised form of rule (absolutism).

During this phase, while playing a significant role in the management of territory-wide frameworks of rule through the *staendisch* bodies, the towns live an intense and varied experience of their own. By and large, they prosper demographically and economically, and in the process they become socially more and more differentiated. Within each town, following the pattern exemplified by the earlier *conjuratio* (the creation of lasting, active solidarities through the mutual agreement of individuals sharing determinate interests), the practitioners of several occupations constitute themselves as distinct corporate bodies, each with statutes and organs of its own. Such bodies secure for their members the monopoly of a given occupation, regulate their productive and commercial practices, and take part on their behalf in the management of town affairs at large. These are entrusted in turn to an increasingly sophisticated structure of town offices (administrative, judicial, and properly political), as well as to the representation of the town's interests in the regional and territorial *Staende*.

For our purposes, what most deserves emphasis in these developments is the peculiar nature of the occupational groupings mentioned above, and of the relative organisation forms (corporations, guilds, etc.). We may designate each such grouping – in another meaning of an unfortunately polysemic term of which Weber makes much use – as a *Stand* or 'estate'. In a sense, *all* townsmen make up *single* estate, comprising all those individuals (or, rather, all those male heads of households) who having been born in the town or having lived and worked (and perhaps owned property) there for more than so many months, now enjoy the status of townsmen, and as such live under the town's laws, enjoy the town's franchises, and are subject to the fiscal and military burdens of citizenship. The intensified division of labour characteristic of this second phase, however, progressively attributes more significance to the townsmen's membership in narrower, occupation-based estates than to their citizenship as such.

As we have seen, the corporate organs of the several occupations set and enforce rules for their practice (affecting sometimes not just their members, but also their customers). They also control other aspects of the member's existence: for instance, matters of cult or dress, consumption practices and leisure activities. Their essential concern, however, is to regulate their occupational activities in such a way as to minimise encroachment upon them by non-members, and maximise the members' returns from them.

Since such bodies confer on individuals exclusive, legally recognised, advantageous and potentially invidious claims, membership in each is open primarily to their members' descendants. Even these, however, have to undergo protracted occupational training and social initiation before they can gain full membership. The exclusive nature of the body, the semi-hereditary basis of membership, the pervasiveness of the regulations controlling the members' existence – all these features sustain in members a keen sense of belonging, a diffuse solidarity with one another, an attachment to those traditional practices in which they have all been trained, and whose respect prevents competition between members.

These features of the typical occupation-based urban estate engender *between* them tendencies toward estrangement and rivalry. These can be contained as long as all such groupings share a strong, overriding attachment to the town itself, and when involved in the management of its affairs loyally pursue in the first place the interests of the whole town. However, during the period we are considering, the power of the territory's central ruler generally increases (as we have seen, mostly with the support of the town element itself); as a result, the towns become less and less concerned with the political and military activities concerning the territory at large, which are increasingly left to the central ruler. Thus the government of the town itself becomes more and more concerned with the management of increasing rivalries and tensions between the occupational groupings – or, rather, between the respective leading elements. For progessively a form of strictly economic differentiation has superimposed itself upon inter-occupational differentiation; there is an increasing distinction (and tension), within each occupation, between the more established and affluent members, and those living a more precarious existence (a distinction that overlaps in part with that between masters and journeymen).

Conflicts *within* and conflict *between* occupational estates inter-sect with varying outcomes. But one of the more common and lasting effects is the emergence, across the occupational divisions of the urban social structure, of relatively solidary and 'estate con-scious' middle and upper strata, constituted by the more prosperous traders and master craftsmen, of whatever occupation.

This is the burgher estate which, as I interpret the two passages from the *Vorbemerkung* quoted above (p. 94), constitutes the first collective identity of the Western *Buergertum*. Its members hold more extensive property; the economic activities carried out within their households and its adjuncts employ more dependants and have a bigger turnover than those of their 'occupational brethren'. For many purposes these similarities become more significant than the occupational identities differentiating this stratum, and ground among its constituents an 'estate solidarity', which is affirmed in the way they live, dress, and consume, and in whose name they some-times usurp from the citizenship at large the exclusive access to certain urban offices.

A final aspect of this phase deserves mention: the extensive and creative explorations of new institutional, intellectual, and aesthetic horizons undertaken by the citizens of the late-medieval/early-modern towns. Weber's references to these explorations emphasise the resultant trend toward the intellectualisation of experience, associated with the growth of literacy in the towns, and particularly in their middle and upper strata.

In the religious sphere, the towns' cathedrals and chapters supplant the monasteries (normally located in the coutryside) as the main institutional centres of Christianity; and also the more signifi-cant new religious orders have prevalently an urban location and orientation. Largely within these new settings, two important relig-ious developments take place. Christian theology receives sophisti-cated, systematic elaboration, chiefly at the hands of scholastic theologians and philosophers (many of them active in the town-based universities). And, increasingly, the practice of piety and morals lays new emphasis on subjective processes internal to the individual conscience.

Several writings of Weber's examine at length, sometimes in technical terms, two important developments in the sphere of law.[5] In the first place, the rediscovery and close study of Roman law (together with the systematisation of canon law) lay the premises of a tradition of rigorous juridical thinking which is to last for centuries and have extensive effects on Continental legal practice. In the second place, imaginative new legal arrangements are devised for the practice of trade and particularly for the formation of business partnerships. According to Weber, both developments express the intellectual and pragmatic tendencies of the burgher element, with its need for forms of law that would rationalise adjudication and thus secure and make calculable economic transactions. He also stresses the creative role played (particularly on the Continent) by a distinctive section of the burgher estate, the university-trained, professional lawyers, judges and jurists.

In the political sphere, significant institutional innovations affect the formal representation of different social bodies both in the *Staendestaat* and in town government, and the formation of systems of councils and offices for the governance of the town. Perhaps Weber underplays somewhat the significance of the latter experience as a precedent for the later development of state-wide bureaucratic systems, stressing instead the examples constituted by the internal arrangements of the Church and the army. He acknowledges, however, that the nature and intensity of social conflict in the towns, and some of the arrangements made in the town polity to control such conflict, prefigure the later experiences of larger states in the face of the class struggle.

As far as I know, Weber does not discuss at length the innovations in the patterning of social intercourse, in the relations between the sexes, in the arrangement of social space and social time, associated with the high density of urban settlements and with the advance of social differentiation in the late-medieval town. According to later sociologists, however, his references to these topics suggest his awareness of the deep and pervasive significance of the town experience in this connection.[6]

Finally, Weber discusses at various points the multiple and sometimes revolutionary aesthetic innovations associated with town life, and particularly with the style of life of the wealthier burghers and the resultant activities of artists and literati. In his view, however, many of those innovations convey the upper burgher estate's tendency to imitate the life patterns and the aesthetic predilections of the feudal nobility. As we shall see, within the next phase in its story the Western *Buergertum* (or at any rate significant sections of it) loosened the lien that the feudal way of life had maintained for centuries upon the imagination and aspirations of the economically more fortunate upper urban strata.

This third phase in the story sees a shift in the social identity of some middle and upper-middle groups from that of an estate (or cluster of estates) to that of a class. The argument in *The Protestant Ethic*, I submit, concerns one distinctive and significant aspect of this fundamental transformation.

In the political sphere, a trend already mentioned above makes further, decisive advances during this phase. The authority of central rulers becomes consolidated over wider territories, and decreases the political significance of the institutions of the *Staendestaat*. Their participation in those institutions still affords the privileged groups (the feudal element, the clergy, the towns) a useful public validation of their privileges; but they intervene less frequently and effectively in the political management of the wider systems of rule. Rather, both the feudal and the town element put their privileges to use in maintaining their economic advantage and their social standing at the local level, respectively over the rural and over the town populace.

In particular, as the central ruler progressively extends his own prerogatives (for instance, by building up territory-wide arrangements for protecting and policing the land, adjudicating controversies, collecting tribute) the towns need concern themselves less and less with maintaining their juridical autonomy and military strength. Furthermore, some rulers undertake to codify, uniformise, and sanction those regulations of commercial and productive activities originally produced within the towns; the pursuit of those activities, as a consequence, no longer requires the towns to maintain their separate jurisdictional powers. Thus in urban political life the town's political autonomy at large becomes less significant than the rivalries between lineages and factions, or the increasing contrasts between the upper, middle, and lower urban strata over the town's economic policies and the allocation of its governmental offices.

But the existence of increasingly wide and secure frameworks of rules for the conduct of commercial and productive activities also made it possible for some urban groups to enter – indeed, to initiate – a wholly novel economic game. A number of individual businessmen undertook to exploit the opportunities opened up by a variety of new developments: the acceleration of traffics caused by the expanding reach of the European economy and of the European states system; the existence of sizeable numbers of property-less labourers both in the towns and in the countryside; the surging demand for some manufactured products; the availability of new productive and accounting techniques. In response to these opportunities some businessmen mobilised (part of) their patrimonies, modified their business practices, and transformed their relations to their dependants, their customers, their families, their locality. While carrying out such innovations in order to generate profits and accumulate capital, they also modified deeply and irreversibly their relations to one another, to their previous occupational identities, and to the related estate affiliations. The outcome of these protracted and locally differentiated transformations was a new historical embodiment of the *Buergertum* – the bourgeois class.

In *The Protestant Ethic* Weber emphasises two specific (though overlapping) aspects of these developments, generating a distinctive new mental and moral habitus in those sections of the *Buergertum* that led the others in economic modernisation: a process of individualisation; and a process of rationalisation. This emphasis is legitimate, but should not obscure some *continuities* between the earlier burgher estate(s) and the latter bourgeoisie – continuities significant enough, in my view, to justify us considering the latter a transformation of the former, not an utterly novel historical actor.

That a process of individualisation is involved is clear; for a class is not a corporate entity, but a looser aggregation of individuals each operating autonomously and on behalf of his own interest, though *de facto* directed in those operations also by *shared* interests. However, a distant premise of this process may be seen in a certain duality of moral and intellectual capacities already present in the earliest protagonists of the Western town experience. For, from the beginning, each townsman was, on the one hand, a *socius*: insignificant by himself, in a landscape dominated by the feudal *potentes*, he could only matter in so far as he joined up with other, equally insignificant fellow townsmen to form a collective, corporate *potens*. On the other hand, each townsman was determined to be his own man. The very point of joining up with others in dangerous and subversive military and political undertakings was for him primarily to establish the town as a juridical enclave, a place where he could attend safely, steadily, and gainfully, to the unheroic, mundane pursuit of a trade or craft. It is on this account that medieval towns worked out ways of transacting political and administrative affairs on a continuous basis through a system of offices, while involving the individual townsmen only intermittently. For – unlike the members of the Greek *polis* – the townsmen wanted to expend most of their energies not in the public square, but each attending to his own business in his *bottega* or *kontor* or on the road from one fair to another. Of course, trade and craft practices came to be thoroughly regulated by occupational estates. But such regulations, and the resultant identification of estate members with their occupational brethren, presupposed the abiding interest of each in his own and his family's welfare, and furthered that interest in order to keep it from finding expression in competition.

As far as the process of rationalisation was concerned, then, we should be aware that a certain rationalism had always marked the townsman's existence, as must be apparent from our brief review of the cultural accomplishments of the burgher estate during the previous phase. However, that rationalism had largely taken the form of the systematisation and further conceptual elaboration of bodies of intellectual material considered as embodying God's revelation and perennial wisdom: the Scriptures and the millenial Church tradition; the legacy of Greek philosophy; Roman law as re-ordered by Justinian; the corpus of classical literature in the process of being rediscovered by the humanists. In dealing with such materials, rationalism was constantly tempered and bounded by traditionalism – in the same way that the townsman's individualism was tempered and bounded by his solidarity with his occupational brethren and by their shared attachment to the corporation's traditions (49; *58–9*).

On these structural and cultural restraints upon individualism and rationalism largely depended the maintenance of the estate structure of the early modern Western town. But the processes discussed in *The Protestant Ethic and the Spirit of Capitalism* acted as a powerful solvent on such restraints; they helped undermine the estate affiliations of the individuals they affected, allowing them to devise new undertakings whose long-run success was to make the estate structure obsolete, and allow some of its components to form themselves into a new social entity, a class.

Let us construct, from Weber's maddeningly few and meagre suggestions (e.g. 55, 262 f256; *65, 272 f62*) an outline account of the events involved. The religious revolution we call Reformation takes place while (in our schematic narrative) the Western *Buergertum* is in the third phase of its story. Through complex developments in which both structural conditions and sheer historical contingencies play a part, different regions in Europe respond differently to the contending creeds and religious bodies, some abiding by the Roman faith, others going over to this or that Protestant confession (269 f277; *277–8 f84*). In a number of regions, religious affiliations differ also between social groups; and all the more so in the towns, given their greater social differentation and literacy.

According to Weber, in those areas where Calvinism attains its greatest diffusion (Switzerland, the Low Countries, England, Scotland) it is particularly the *urban middle and lower-middle strata* – in so far as they exist; which is not very far in the case of Scotland[7] – that respond to this belief (152; *139*). It was then primarily within these groups, *already* occupationally involved in business, that -- over a generation or two – the causal sequence Calvinist doctrine → inner-worldly asceticism → spirit of capitalism added its own effects to other factors facilitating the transition to the capitalist conduct of business (272 f286; *279 f93*).

Individuals motivated by the particular urgency of religious convictions and the attendant moral concerns were more likely to loosen their bonds to their associates, and to question the validity of traditional constraints on economic activity (36; *42–3*). For those possessing the requisite resources and skills for doing business in the new, capitalist way, the thoroughgoing individualisation of their moral horizons acted as an additional, critical incentive.

The traditional locus of business activity was the household, of which the shop or counting-house was a part or adjunct. The master's relations to his dependants did not differ drastically, in emotional tone and in the patterning of interaction (chiefly through his own patriarchal dominance), from those to his family members. As the wider meaning of the term *familia* itself indicates (it comprised domestic servants and sometimes other dependants), the bonds of blood and affinity often overlapped with those tying together the personnel operating a business; and, as we have seen, entry into an occupation was largely a hereditary matter, or followed a training prolonged and intense enough to resemble initiation into a semi-familial bond. Work and leisure activity often had the same locales and overlapped in time, and both involved one with the same set of associates. In running the business, its head did not distinguish its assets and the returns from their employment from his family patrimony and its revenues. The target of business activity and the criterion of its success was the ability to provide regularly for the family's needs, in so far as these corresponded with the style of life, the consumption standards, etc., publicly recognised as appropriate to the family's estate and to its social standing in the town.

Estate regulations and traditions had as their referent *this* complex of activities and expectations, with their emphasis on proximity, persistence, familiarity. By thrusting the individual upon himself, Calvinism loosens up that complex, and assists in the formation of new social relations, outside the reach of estate regulations and traditions. As the entrepreneur finds his workers among the increasing number of property-less individuals in town and countryside (who often work in their own home), the locus of business activity becomes detached from the household. Since the entrepreneur often relies on credit, he finds it necessary to separate the accounts dealing with loaned funds and other business resources (and their returns) from those concerning his personal and family funds and expenditures.

In making business decisions, the entrepreneur must increasingly bypass or directly contravene the rules of the occupational bodies concerning commercial and productive practices. For, those rules, as we have seen, protected estate solidarity by restraining competition; but competition is the name of the new economic game, which can only be played by violating those rules and surrendering the attendant solidarities.

On other counts, too, are the estate bonds weakened. In the light of the new understanding of what makes an individual's life morally worthy – the mastery of his calling as an end to itself – the estate's other main preoccupation, the regulation not of work but of life-style (attire, consumption, possessions, modalities of status display), appears to foster an irresponsible concern with irrelevant externalities and to hinder capital accumulation by endless expenditure. Also, the reach of estate solidarities could not extend beyond the single town, for only here could individuals sustain relations marked (as estate relations must be marked) by physical proximity, personal acquaintance, and a degree of emotional intensity. Now, however, the entrepreneur stands at the intersection of multiple markets, where he acquires his production factors and disposes of his products; both kinds of markets extend over wider and wider territories, encompass a number of towns. Thus, the entrepreneur must operate in the actual or potential presence of innumerable strangers, in their capacity as suppliers, customers, competitors, workers. In manoeuvring himself over this wider, open-ended social space, he cannot rely on the trust generated by personal acquaintance, fellow feeling, shared orientation to tradition. If he is to win trust, he must do so through the scrupulous observance of formal legal obligations.

Thus the third phase of our story sees the progressive erosion – aided *also* by impulses originating in the religious sphere – of those affiliations that in the previous phase moderated the burgher's abiding commitment to (as I have phrased it) being his own man. A powerful, because relatively unconstrained, process of individualisation now reshapes the entrepreneur's relationship to his business associates, his family, himself. The novel ethical component of this new set of relationships, according to Weber, is the individual's sense of *personal responsibility*. It is the essence of the *Berufsmensch* that he does not distance himself from his occupational task, treat it as a mere facility or adjunct of his person, but is willing to stand or fall as a whole person by its results, rather than imputing them to blind forces or to God's favour or disfavour. In this sense, Weber argues, inner-worldly asceticism grounds the notion itself of *personality* as a self-activating centre of initiative, the locus of a silent dialogue whereby the individual sets himself against the outside world and commits his whole self to controlling that world, thereby testing his inner worth.

In this third phase also the equilibrium previously achieved between rationality and tradition is undermined. The relevant concrete processes largely coincide with those already described; for the estate affiliations served not only to maintain solidarities, but also to convey and to sanction traditional expectations; thus their erosion both causes and is caused by an increasing reliance upon deliberate rational choice in the conduct of business activity.

We may visualise individualisation as removing the *spatial* constraints shaping the business experience in its pre-capitalist phases: the locus of production tends to shift away from the household, the entrepreneur seeks his factors of production and disposes of his products over wider, translocal markets, etc. The new modes of rationality, unbounded by tradition, may then appear to break through the *temporal* constraints upon business as conducted in the old manner. Entrepreneurial choice no longer legitimises itself by its actual or claimed continuity with the past or fidelity to its inspiration. It treats the past as contingent, and its results as resources or obstacles, to be circumvented or put to use in pressing forward to ever-new results. Rationality thus becomes ruthlessly dynamic: it problematises every arrangement, seeks to surpass every achievement. Concretely, the new logic of entrepreneurial activity is oriented to endless accumulation, not to the provision of resources for direct enjoyment or aesthetic or status display. In this, the new rationality, by disconnecting its aims from the justification or the standards offered by felt human needs, reveals more clearly than other forms of rationality a paradox common to all, according to Weber: their ultimately irrational character (see Chapter 4).

In characterising this third phase in the development of the Western *Buergertum*, I have so far emphasised the erosion of its collective identity as an estate by the associated processes of individualisation and rationalisation (both assisted by the religious and ethical developments examined by Weber in *The Protestant Ethic*). This emphasis now needs to be corrected by a few complementary remarks.

In the first place, those processes do not only undermine the estate affiliations of their protagonists; they also generate their new collective identity as the bourgeois class. The commitment to profit and accumulation, the necessity of dealing with competitive threats, the demands of building up and managing the firm – all these requirements impose upon the entrepreneur's existence constraints more objective and abstract, and publicly less validated, than those associated with estate memberships, but no less cogent and less capable of sustaining a collective identity. To the same effect operates the position entrepreneurs share as employers; for, as he buys labour on the market and organises its performance with a view to his own managerial control, each entrepreneur unavoidably generates in his workers interests in contrast with his own, which in turn are no longer shaped and moderated by estate regulations. The confrontation with these antagonistic interests generates an active solidarity among the entrepreneurs, although they can no longer appeal to publicly recognised political privileges in imposing their superiority, and although their solidarity, being largely mediated through the market, is muted and often invisible.

In the second place, at any rate in their earlier phases the processes of individualiation and rationalisation we have discussed involve only a section, possibly a minor one, within the property-owning, business *Buergertum*. For quite some time the majority probably sought to go on practising (literally) 'business as usual' – until the success of the new entrepreneurship changed the name of everybody's game, and the class form of collective identity widened its reach correspondingly. In fact, as late as the first part of the nineteenth century, Max Weber's own paternal grandfather had gone on practising his business as a textile manufacturer after an *archaic*, premodern capitalist pattern; and only his successor in the headship of the family firm, Max's uncle, David Carl, had thoroughly modernised its business practices. It is on the latter episode of recent family history that Weber based a lively, narrative account of the difference the *spirit* of capitalism had made to traditional *forms* of capitalist enterprise (55–8; *66–8*).

Thirdly, while I would insist that the contrast between estate and class defines the proper *conceptual* space within which to inscribe the processes discussed in *The Protestant Ethic*, it is important not to overstate the *empirical* significance of that contrast. It is characteristic of estate (as against class) affiliations that they impose on members a certain style of life. But as they disaffiliated themselves from their own estate(s), the entrepreneurs themselves could not but adopt a new, distinctive style of life. This style of course no longer embodies an exclusively, publicly valid claim to estate privileges, and does not arise from compliance with estate rules; rather, it expresses the intensity of the entrepreneurs' commitment to their calling, of their ethically motivated submission to the demands of profit-making and of class interest; and it reflects a primary preoccupation with the accumulation rather than the expenditures of resources (172; *163*). It *is*, for all that, a style of life of which Weber emphasises the sobriety, solidity, and austerity, coherent with the Calvinist understanding of existence and the self. Thus, in a sense, in the very process of becoming a class, this section of the *Buergertum* unavoidably restyles itself as an estate of a new kind, characterised by its refusal to ape the noble pattern of existence, and by its adoption of what we would today call a 'low profile' (179–80; *171*).

Finally, the transformation I have been discussing, even when it affects wider groups than those who had initiated it, did not affect uniformly all locales of social existence. As I have indicated, the new class bonds are intrinsically translocal, and operate chiefly by means of the market, that is (for a long time) prevalently at the regional and national level. As such, they allow estate-like forms of consciousness and patterns of interaction to remain in operation at the local level, on the basis of personal acquaintance, connubial 'alliances' and the resultant kinship ties, extensive sociable inter-course, often the self-conscious cultivation of the town's distinctive linguistic, cultural, and historical heritage. On these grounds, the Western town (and then city) remains for a long time the habitat of a number of relatively archaic, estate-type groupings of bourgeois elements – witness, Thomas Mann's *Buddenbrooks*.

I shall sum up again the reading of *The Protestant Ethic* proposed in this chapter. During the third phase in the history of the Western *Buergertum*, some burgher groups involved in business, *and* whose members had been for a generation or two brought up in the Calvinist creed, derived from the distinctive content of that creed, through the complex mediations we have reviewed in Chapter 6, an ascetic orientation to their occupation. As a consequence they adopted a new, energetic and innovative approach to their business activities, which allowed them to play the leading role in promoting the modern capitalist mode of production. At the same time and for the same reasons, that approach loosened up for such elements the bonds to their estate associates, and caused the related constraints upon their occupational activities to lose significance and to become discarded. Their intense commitment to their *Beruf* no longer entailed the occupancy of a stable corporate position within a visible, publicly recognised, orderly status structure; it had become instead, to each entrepreneur, more like an open-ended script, offering him a chance to prove his moral worth (and thus, indirectly and implicitly, his condition as an elect) in the strenuous pursuit of profit through the rational utilisation of his capital assets.

Since that pursuit took place through competition over increasingly wide and open markets, its protagonists typically became isolated from one another, or maintained sociable ties (originating largely from their previous mutual affiliations as estate members) only at the local level. Meanwhile, at the translocal level there came into being between entrepreneurs a solidarity of a new type, based on the factual interests they shared as owners of the means of production and buyers of labour power. Thus the Western *Buergertum* went on to a new phase in its history, in the new collective identity of a class.

At the beginning of this book, and again at the beginning of this final chapter, I have suggested that for Weber the Western *Buergertum* constituted both a wider collective entity of which he personally felt a part, and the explicit or implicit theme of sustained inquiry in a number of diverse writings. Among the latter I have drawn on 'The City' in order to show how Weber differentiated *diachronically* that collective entity, and suggested that *The Protestant Ethic* deals with a critical aspect of one major phase within the *Buergertum*'s story.

But Weber differentiates that object in other ways, two of which deserve mention. In the first place (as I have briefly indicated in this chapter) the *Buergertum* appears as *hierarchically* differentiated, in the sense that through most of its history it is composed of a small number of sub-units which stand to one another more or less visibly as superior or inferior in terms of social power (in its various dimensions: wealth, status, rulership), and which periodically contend over the allocation of social power. Early on, the sub-units in question are chiefly occupational estates, to which the town's status structure assigns a precise rank within a publicly sanctioned array of positions. Later, a more distinctively economic system of urban strata comes to superimpose itself upon that array. In this system the uppermost stratum is constituted by the wealthier and more successful masters within any occupational estate; under this lies a stratum of less wealthy and successful masters, and next the journeymen of any occupation. An increasingly wide stratum of semi-proletarianised townsmen 'without art or part', as one says in Italian, occupies the bottom position. Subsequently, according to Weber, it is chiefly within the member of the second, intermediate stratum that the processes discussed in *The Protestant Ethic* work their effects, and (together, of course, with a host of other factors) produce in the long run a new kind of market-based stratification system; here the top stratum is constituted by the newly emerged bourgeois class.

In the second place, Weber differentiated various sections of the

Western *Buergertum* in terms of their distinctive involvements in one or the other of several spheres of social and cultural experience. Thus, while *The Protestant Ethic* deals specifically with (some aspects of the formation of) the entrepreneurial section of the *Buergertum* and its strategic contribution to the development of the modern economic order, other writings of Weber's deal implicitly or explicitly with other sections of the *Buergertum* and their distinctive pursuits: chiefly, lawyers (both academic jurists on the one hand and attorneys and judges on the other); bureaucrats; intellectuals; scientists and scholars; artists; religious thinkers and leaders; politicians. Of course Weber does not impute exclusively to each of these sections of the *Buergertum* the distinctive Western achievements in the respective spheres of cultural and social experience. It is clear to him, for instance, that in the early, decisive phases of Western state-building, and particularly in the related military and diplomatic undertakings, the leading role was played by personnel of princely or aristocractic extraction, and that only later (first as administrators, then as politicians) burgher/bourgeois personnel came to perform critical political functions. It is also clear that while a majority of the creative Western legal thinkers have been of burgher/bourgeois extraction, the Roman jurists (both late-republican and imperial) who had worked out previously both the methodology and the basic substantive principles of the Western juridical heritage, could not themselves, by any stretch of the imagination, be considered part of the Western *Buergertum*. However, wherever Weber characterises the specific Western developments of this or that major sphere of social or cultural experience, many of the typical bodies of personnel he evokes as the protagonists of each development constitute one or another section of the Western *Buergertum*, each differentiated in terms of its distinctive skills and preoccupations. No matter how much they differ in other terms, the priests and theologians, the lawyers, the journalists, the politicians, the university professors, the functionaries of public and private bureaucracies, the artists and musicians, the stock-jobbers, and the bankers, who people Weber's pages, often have in common with one another, *and with the entrepreneurs*, their membership in one larger social entity – the Western *Buergertum*.

If, as I have just suggested, the latter entity is differentiated by Weber along three dimensions – in terms of phases of development, in terms of internal stratification, in terms of distinctive bodies of personnel – one may then 'triangulate' the argument in *The Protestant Ethic and the Spirit of Capitalism* by using those same dimensions. In terms of the last differentiation proposed, that essay deals exclusively with one section of the *Buergertum*: that involved in business. In terms of hierarchical differentiation, it deals with a *middle* stratum in the process of becoming an *upper* one by changing the rules of the economic game and thus subverting the estate system of stratification. Finally, in terms of diachronic differentiation, *The Protestant Ethic* bears upon what I have called the third phase in the story of the *Buergertum*.

This chapter has developed at some length only this last characterisation of Weber's argument in *The Protestant Ethic*. The task of justifying and developing the other characterisations may be left to further inquiries.

Notes and References

Preface

1. The key texts have been assembled by Johannes Winckelmann in: Max Weber, *Die protestantische Ethik. II: Kritiken und Antikritiken* (Munich: Siebenstern, 1968). Some other useful critiques and commentaries are assembled, often in much shortened versions, in R. W. Green (ed.), *Protestantism and Capitalism: The Weber Thesis and its Critics* (Boston: Heath, 1961). The recent book by G. Marshall, *In Search of The Spirit of Capitalism: An Essay on Max Weber's Protestant Ethic Thesis* (London: Hutchinson, 1982) presents the best review and assessment to date of the controversy. Two previous, notable attempts in this direction are: L. Cavalli, *Max Weber: Religione e società* (Bologna: Mulino, 1968); J. A. Prades, *La sociologie de la religion chez Max Weber* (Louvain: Nauwelaerts, 1969).

2. Just one example: J. A. Winter, 'Elective Affinities between Religious Beliefs and Ideologies of Management in Two Eras', *American Journal of Sociology*, 79 (March 1974) 1134–50. At p. 1138 the author writes, by way of summary of the position taken by Weber in *The Protestant Ethic*:

> There is, then, an elective affinity between the religious beliefs which constitute the Protestant Ethic, with its concept of predestination, and the spirit of [early] capitalism, the entrepreneurial ideology. A belief in predestination provided, through its linkage to the concept of the calling, an expression of the 'essence and strivings' of the entrepreneur, his desire for profit, his commitment to success in business.

This is not, as such things go, a *particularly* inadequate rendering of Weber's argument. Yet note that religious beliefs are said to 'constitute' the Protestant ethic – whereas, as I shall endeavour to show (in Chapter 5 particularly), Weber posits a contingent relationship between two entities, a set of *religious* beliefs at one end and a set of *ethical* ideas at the other. The 'concept' of predestination is *not* a property, or aspect, of the Protestant ethic, but of Calvinist dogma. Belief in predestination did not *express* the entrepreneur's desire for profit, but if anything indirectly *motivated* it – which is a rather different relationship.

3. I am referring to the writings by Max Weber known in English as *The*

Religion of China: Confucianism and Taoism; *Ancient Judaism*; *The Religion of India: The Sociology of Induism and Buddhism*. These texts were all published by The Free Press of Glencoe, Illinois, respectively in 1951, 1952 and 1958. (The translations are not always reliable.) The original Weberian texts are put to excellent use, together with others, in W. Schluchter, *The Rise of Western Rationalism: Max Weber's Developmental History*, translated, with an Introduction, by Guenther Roth (Berkeley: University of California Press, 1981).

4. Marshall, *In Search of the Spirit of Capitalism*.

Chapter 1

1. Marianne Weber, *Max Weber: A Biography* (New York: Wiley, 1975). The original text was published in 1926.

2. See, for example: W. J. Mommsen, *Max Weber und die deutsche Politik, 1890–1920* (Tuebingen: Mohr, 1959); E. Baumgarten (ed.), *Max Weber: Werk und Person* (Tuebingen: Mohr, 1964); A. Mitzman, *The Iron Cage* (New York: Knopf, 1970); D. Kaesler, 'Max Weber', in D. Kaesler (ed.), *Klassiker des soziologischen Denkens* (Munich: Beck, 1978) II, 40–177.

3. See the bibliography appended to Kaesler, 'Max Weber', pp. 425–46.

4. See G. Roth, 'Introduction' to Max Weber, *Economy and Society* (Totowa, N. J.: Bedminster, 1968) I, LXX–LXXI.

5. W. Sombart, *Der moderne Kapitalismus* (Leipzig: Duncker & Humblot, 1902).

6. On this, see J. A. Smith, 'The Protestant Ethic Controversy', unpublished Ph.D. thesis (University of Cambridge, 1981).

7. Roth, 'Introduction' to Weber, *Economy and Society*, p. XXIX.

8. See the texts collected by J. Wincklemann in: Max Weber, *Die protestantische Ethik, II: Kritiken und Antikritiken* (Munich: Siebenstern, 1968).

9. See, for instance, the editors' Introduction to H. Gerth and C. W. Mills (eds), *From Max Weber: Essays in Sociology* (New York: Oxford University Press, 1974) 23.

10. J. Weiss, *Max Webers Grundlegung der Soziologie* (Munich: Documentation, 1975). My discussion follows closely Weiss's treatment of this topic.

11. Gerth and Mills, *From Max Weber*, 217–18.

12. See, in particular, P. Honigsheim, *On Max Weber* (New York: Free Press, 1968).

13. K.-S. Rehberg, 'Rationales Handeln als grossbuergerliches Aktionsmodell: Thesen zu einigen handlungstheoretischen Implikationen der "Soziologischen Grundbegriffe" Max Webers' *Koelner Zeitschrift f. Soziologie und Sozialpsychologie*, 31 (1979) 199–236. The quote is from p. 217.

14. G. Roth, 'Max Weber's Generational Rebellion and Maturation', in R. Bendix and G. Roth, *Scholarship and Partisanship: Essays on Max Weber* (Berkeley: University of California Press, 1971) 18–19.

Chapter 2

1. C. E. Lindblom, *Politics and Markets: The World's Political-Economic Systems* (New York: Basic Books, 1975). Among the previous authors emphasising 'interaction' as the primary mechanism of a capitalist economy, see O. Hintze, 'Economics and Politics in the Age of Modern Capitalism', in *The Historical Essays of Otto Hintze* (New York: Oxford University Press, 1975) 428.

2. See J. Winckelmann, in Max Weber, *Wirtschaft und Gesellschaft* (Tuebingen: Mohr, 1976) vol. III, p. 101, *sub* p. 369.

3. Ibid, p. 103, again *sub* 369.

4. *General Economic History* omits to translate the opening chapter of *Wirtschaftsgeschichte* from which this passage is taken.

Chapter 3

1. Notice, however, the good use to which this text has recently been put by Randall Collins, in 'Weber's Last Theory of Capitalism: A Systematization', *American Sociological Review*, 45 (1980) 925–42.

2. Relevant reflections have been developed in an interesting essay by Randall Collins, 'A Comparative Approach to Political Sociology', in R. Bendix (ed.), *State and Society* (Boston: Little, Brown, 1968) 42–67.

3. This point has been effectively emphasised in W. M. Sprondel, 'Sozialer Wandel, Ideen und Interessen: Systematisierungen zu Max Webers Protestantische Ethik', in C. Seyfarth and W. M. Sprondel (eds), *Seminar: Religion und gesellschaftliche Entwicklung* (Frankfurt: Suhrkamp, 1973) esp. 214.

Chapter 4

1. H. Gerth and C. W. Mills (eds), *From Max Weber: Essays in Sociology* (New York: Oxford University Press, 1947) 280.

2. Reinhard Bendix's treatment of these studies in his *Max Weber: An Intellectual Portrait* (New York: Doubleday, 1960) Part Two, remains the best critical survey of a vast and demanding body of materials.

Chapter 5

1. This point is impressively documented in the opening chapters of J. A. Smith, 'The Protestant Ethic Controversy', unpublished Ph.D. thesis (University of Cambridge, 1981).

Chapter 6

1. 'The Protestant Sects and the Spirit of Capitalism', in H. Gerth and C. W. Mills (eds), *From Max Weber: Essays in Sociology* (New York: Oxford University Press, 1947) 220.

2. An interesting exploration of the significance of the metaphor of 'affinity' in Weber's thinking is offered in R. H. Howe, 'Max Weber's Elective Affinities: Sociology Within the Bounds of Pure Reason', *American Journal of Sociology*, 84 (1978) 366–85.

3. S. D. Berger, 'The Sects and the Breakthrough into the Modern World: On the Centrality of the Sects in Weber's Protestant Ethic Thesis', *Sociological Quarterly*, 12 (1971) 486–99, has justly emphasised the significance of this essay.

4. 'The Protestant Sects', p. 219.

Chapter 7

1. The indispensability of such alternative approaches, and the difficulties they imply, are at the centre of the thoughtful critical reconstruction of Weber's own argument offered in G. Marshall, *In Search of the Spirit of Capitalism: An Essay on Max Weber's Protestant Ethic Thesis* (London: Hutchinson, 1982). See esp. ch. 5, 'The Heart of the Matter'.

2. See, for example, A. Giddens, 'Marx, Weber and the Development of Capitalism', in A. Giddens, *Studies in Social and Political Theory* (London: Hutchinson, 1977) 183–202. On other issues connected with 'Marx *v.* Weber' see V.-M. Bader *et al.*, *Einfuehrung in die Gesellschaftstheorie: Gesellschaft, Wirtschaft und Staat bei Marx und Weber*, 2 vols (Frankfurt: Campus, 1976).

3. See, for instance, D. McLellan (ed.), *Karl Marx: Selected Writings* (London: Macmillan, 1977) 388–92.

4. I borrow this expression from Helmuth Plessner's philosophical anthropology; see, for instance, his 'Ueber einige Motive der philosophischen Anthropologie', *Studium Generale*, 9 (1956) 445–60.

5. See, for instance, W. Schluchter, *The Rise of Western Nationalism: Max Weber's Developmental History* (Berkeley: University of California Press, 1981).

Chapter 8

1. Personal communication to the author from Guenther Roth.

2. Already R. Bendix, *Max Weber: An Intellectual Portrait* (New York: Doubleday, 1960) 92ff. had seen the bearing of *The Protestant Ethic* on the

(apparently rather different) Weberian theme of the peculiarities of the Western urban experience.

3. See W. M. Sprondel, 'Sozialer Wandel, Ideen und Interessen: Systematisierungen zu Max Webers Protestantische Ethik', in C. Seyfarth and W. M. Sprondel (eds), *Seminar: Religion und gesellschaftliche Entwicklung* (Frankfurt: Suhrkamp, 1973) 213–14.

4. Max Weber, *Gesammelte Politische Schriften*, 2nd edn (Tuebingen: Mohr, 1958) 20. For a partial translation of Weber's inaugural, containing the passage referred to here, see Max Weber, *Selections in Translation*, edited by W. G. Runciman (Cambridge: Cambridge University Press, 1978) 263–68.

5. See 'Economy and Law (Sociology of Law)', ch. VIII of Max Weber, *Economy and Society* (Totowa, N. J.: Bedminster, 1968) 641–900.

6. H. P. Bahrdt, *Die moderne Grossstadt* (Reinbeck: Rowohlt, 1961) 36–9.

7. The 'Scottish case', and its bearing on the question of the validity of 'Weber thesis', have been thoroughly explored in: G. Marshall, *Presbyteries and Profits: Calvinism and the Development of Capitalism in Scotland, 1560–1707* (Oxford: Oxford University Press, 1980).

Index